Old Spanish proverb:

Traveler, there is no way.
The way is made by going.

HABITS: A JOURNAL

One Womans Struggle Against
Religious Persecution

Wilhelmine Bennett

Habits: A   Journal

First Printing 1998

All of the events herein occurred as
described. Names have been omitted
or changed.

The author is grateful to Blue Mountain
Center for time and space to complete
this manuscript.

Cover design: Marsha Lieberman

Library of Congress Catalogue Card Number
98 - 91560

Published by:
Niangua Press
Greenfield, MA

ISBN :1-57502-892-1

Printed in the USA by

MORRIS PUBLISHING

3212 East Highway 30 • Kearney, NE 68847 • 1-800-650-7888

The rectangular building of painted white shingles has its long axis lying towards the curved street. Relatively free of ornamentation, its simple lines flow uninterrupted along the horizontal, vertically up the steep roof to and over the belfry, and thence to the sky. Four tall narrow windows pierce the long facades at equidistant points. These are framed with Gothic arches which are echoed by the mullions, and contain large squares of glass stained in primary colors. The awkward effect of this crude rendering however, is ameliorated and finally overcome by the graceful proportions of the whole: windows to wall, wall to roof, belfry to roof, the gestalt inducing a pleasant feeling of lightness and delicacy.

Two constructions mar this effect. First is an addition to the back of the building whose roof angle neither duplicates nor departs sufficiently from that of the church proper, hence defys integration; unfelicitous too is the shape, size, and placement of the windows in this section. Missing are the graceful relationships worked out (or fortuitously arrived at) for the Gothic windows. The second blemish is the combined concrete steps and ramp leading to the main entrance. These stairs are steep and of niggardly dimension. Both steps and ramp culminate with a platform, also of niggardly size; a single-peaked roof is placed too high to satisfy aesthetics or practicality. Rain and wind assault the person standing there seeking welcome.

Both of these additions were made during my time there. I watched their construction with dismay.

This Sunday in late May is chilly and the women leaving the church wear sweaters or jackets. The men have on workclothes, worn to a nondescript color, a few wear overalls. As they come out the door no conversational groupings form—whatever social exchanges occur will have taken place during the "coffee hour" following the service in the lower section of the addition. These exchanges have been tearfully described to me by my 12-year-old neighbor girl. But now there are only nods or a few words of closure as they make their way down the steps, some leaning heavily on the bannisters to favor an arthritic knee or ankle. For these are almost exclusively older people though it is hard to assign a precise age. In this village and its surrounds women are frequently toothless by the age of thirty. They also adopt clothes and hairstyles the same as middle-aged housewives, have become obese to a greater or lesser degree, and have mannerisms, gestures and speech inflections common to both those aged twenty-eight or fifty-five. At this latter age, false teeth are purchased though not routinely worn. These cheaply-made, all one-size, ill-fitting dentures, coupled with the matted close-to-the-head gray or graying hair, have the effect of rendering all the women George Washington look-alikes.

The men fare somewhat better. Whether because custom decrees they receive the larger and better portion of food, these men do seem to retain their teeth longer and add replacements before the bone and musculature which defines their physiognomy has eroded. Then too, in this culture men are granted a larger range of expression. Men are the actors; women the acted upon. So even though content and style of action may be limited, men are allowed to retain some idiosyncracies. For the women, a face of passivity is required though the resentment engendered by this imposition might dwell inwardly. These women walking down the church steps will return to their kitchens to finish preparing dinners stuck in the oven before leaving. The men will sit waiting, either impatiently reading the paper or pacing to and fro from their chair to the kitchen doorway, causing the women to hurry and perhaps burn their hand on a dish picked up too hastily. Now they proceed down the steps to get into their pick-up trucks.

Returning from a morning walk, I reckon from a block away that if I continue at the same pace I will be in the midst of these people leaving church. I abruptly turn away.

• • • •

William James warned of the intransigence of small actions which, with repetition, form habits and thence character. That vast biological map, the nervous system, whereby stimuli are processed and converted into response must be stable enough to allow for habit-yet plastic enough to permit learning, Habit as a tendency to repeat with greater ease and precision, can aid and abet the learning process, but the dark side of this equation is that if an action is repeated a number of times (psychologists say thirty-eight) it becomes encapsulated, beyond access. If we put our left shoe on first for a month and eight days, this will come to seem not only right and proper but the only way to don our shoes. We will thus instruct our children who, in turn, will so instruct their children. Perhaps Santanyana meant that we should remember to remember lest we merely repeat. Awareness is all.

In 1870, at the age of 28, James noticed that he could sustain a chosen thought when he might have other thoughts. This validated for him his freedom of volition, saving him from possible suicide. His first act of free will was to believe in free will.

• • • •

3

"You look ... appropriate".

The Director grinned. "Good. I don't have a lot of experience making calls on ministers. I found this skirt and this frilly blouse. Thought I had a bra from twenty years ago— but couldn't find it. So I'll just kinda hunch my shoulders. Look OK?"

"Yeah. In fact, gives you a sort of humble appearance." Nancy replies.

"Have you thought of what you'll say?" asks Ray.

"Well, a lot depends on who he is, I've never even seen him. Basically I'm just approaching it as one reasonable person to another, suggesting a reasonable solution. Can I rehearse it with you?"

Nancy, a poet from California and Ray, a playwright from New York, are current residents at the Colony and don't have much experience negotiating with Baptist ministers. Nor does the Director, though she has lived in their midst long enough to realize there is no guarantee that being "reasonable" will produce good results. In this arena there are mine-fields every place, each step has to be carefully considered.

"Well first, Jesus, how do I address him?"

"Mister? Reverend?" Nancy and Ray speak simultaneously.

"Mister I can manage but Reverend—uh-uh. I think I'll just establish his identity then refrain from using any title. So: I wonder if we can talk about this problem, I mean the problem of the computerized tape."

To Ray, "Is that what it is?"

Ray shrugs. "Its just a tape system with high amplification."

"OK. It's quite loud. QUITE loud and disturbs the residents as well as myself. They aren't able to work, which is their sole reason for being here. So could we compromise by your playing the tape three times daily, like morning, noon, and evening, instead of every half-hour?"

"Huh! Every half-hour and lasting ten minutes so it's really twenty minutes out of each hour," Nancy says angrily. "And maybe you can suggest that instead of hymns they play ... uh, Mozart?"

"Ha ha! Anyway, three times a day with the volume reduced considerably—does that sound OK? Jesus, just think, we're almost a mile away and it's deafening here. Think what it must be like for the poor people who live next door to the church! Well, here I go!"

"Luck!", they both call.

The Director was forgetting to remember. Several years before, in what she had thought was an intellectual discussion about comparative religion with the village librarian, she had said she was a student of Zen Buddhism. Shortly after, her house had been stoned repeatedly for several weeks. Feeling annoyance, not alarm, she had assumed the kids would get bored and desist if they got no response from her. It was only when she discovered they had broken into the new house she was building, had forced the heavy oak doors nailed into their frames to season, and pushed these down onto windows stacked nearby, breaking them, that she recognized the inherent violence and knew she could no longer think of their actions as pranks. But her attempts to identify, in order to confront the guilty ones, were frustrated. Though some in the village admitted knowing about the incidents, no one seemed to know who might be involved. And she had the distinct feeling that not only did they know but that they were pleased. A couple of the kids she questioned told her she'd been stoned because she was a "Zen Buddhist or witch or something."

It all seemed too absurd, the stonings ceased, and all was forgotten. The faint cries of warning went unheeded.

·   ·   ·   ·

It is movement by which most animals attract each others attention. A rabbit who habitually sits quivering when approached by dogs now jumps up and runs as soon as it is aware of the dog's presence. Why this change in behaviour? and will it persevere? Implicit in all learning theories is that certain response-produced effects support or reinforce the response. If the effect of a new response is pleasant or satisfying, Thorndike labels it a reinforcer while Pavlov asserts it is the *strength* of the response which determines its continuance. Not to quibble. In fact, effects become reinforcers when they preserve the response, and when they do not preserve it they are not reinforcers. Hence a habit can be extinguished when reinforcement for it is absent. Obviously the rabbit was not happy with its quivering habit. But if it finds that running from the dog (new response) leads to being caught and mauled, while sticking its ground (old response) merely makes the dog bark at him, will he maintain this new response? Perhaps. Perhaps not. If he persists in running for 38 times (remember?), the potential for learning dwindles. Habituation, (maintaining the same response) however, does have value in that it prevents the organism from continuing to react to something which has proven to be without danger, thereby becoming economical by reducing wear and tear.

· · · ·

It is only 4:35 but she figures if she walks very slowly she will not arrive too far in advance of 5:00. This meeting of the town council has been hard-won after a summer of frustration. On her first visit to the pastor he had been amiable and sympathetic, promising to refer her request to the "bell committee" and to let her know their decision in a couple of weeks. Pleased at the ease of this accomplishment, she had only been slightly startled when, starting to tell him where she lived, he interrupted with "I know where you live". Well, she had reassured herself, in a community of less than three hundred, it was logical he might know this.

A month later, having heard nothing, she visited him again. The pastor was amiable and sympathetic, this time stating that the Bell Committee was doing a survey of the townspeople to determine if others objected. She had resisted pointing out that since the survey was being conducted by Baptists, most in the community were

Baptists, the rest intimidated by Baptists, it could hardly be considered a disinterested survey. Actually, several in the village had indicated to her privately their anger at the bells, but she didn't think they would voice this to the committee. Indeed, she wondered if such a committee existed. Again, no word from the Pastor induced her last visit at which he appeared amiable and sympathetic, telling her the survey revealed only she objected and that her objection would be discussed, a decision made, when next the Bell Comittee met which, unfortunately (he beamed at this) would not be for three months and he would be happy to let her know their decision.

Her next step, she decided, was to determine if there was a town ordinance regarding noise. The town clerk could not locate the ordinance book and referred her to the mayor who referred her to a council member who referred her to another member. It seemed the book had disappeared. Until one morning when she was paying her water bill in the town hall and took advantage of the clerk's engagement in conversation with someone to check the desk drawer, locate the book and copy the proper ordinance. She was delighted to see it was a standard one, worded so as to provide her with a legal weapon.

Next she contacted the town clerk to request a meeting of the council in order to "discuss a possible violation of an ordinance." The town clerk referred her to the mayor who kept "forgetting" to contact council members for a meeting but finally, under her continued pressure, arranged this meeting. The whole process, from her first meeting with the Pastor, had taken six months.

Though she had dawdled, all the while repeating her vow not to be provoked, to refer any and all religious remarks back to the subject at hand, still, when she arrived fifteen minutes early she found all the council members there (she knew hers to be the only item on the agenda) and the subject, though supposedly not yet defined, apparently discussed and already decided.

❂   ❂

The establishment of the artists colony, now in its third year, was a modification of a plan carried over from the director's marriage. During that marriage, she and her husband had traversed the country seeking cheap land and friendly people in order to practice a qualified version of homesteading. They had met in the 70's, and both had missed the Great Migration back to the land of the 60's, he having been involved in the academic and research life of physics, a first marriage and children, while she was consumed with a fulltime job (as psychiatric social worker) and fulltime graduate study (in music composition). While the romantic aspects of that movement held no appeal they had both spent their lives "making things", resolutely independent so the practical components of such a life: building your own house, raising your own food, and whatever other creative ventures pulled at them, were very seductive. After all, she could write music anywhere and since he had decided to "leave" physics (i.e. resign his tenured position at a major university) they were free to follow their desires.

The marriage dissolved before the plan was achieved. But the plan grew in her mind and became even more compelling. So several years later on her first backpacking jaunt in the Ozarks (an area she and her husband had dismissed without exploration), discovering the quiet beauty and unspoiled nature of this area, not to mention the cheapness of the land, the effect was strong enough to offset the uneasiness caused by the religious exhortations blasting her from the car radio. After all, she reasoned, she was hardly an innocent, having been raised as an atheist in similiar Bible-belt country. Her family's marked differences from the community surrounding them, along with their atheism, had placed them in the line of fire and raised a gamut of reactions: respect and resentment, love and fear, jealousy, condescension, envy and disdain. Since she was the youngest of the six children she received the benefit of expert strategies worked out by parents and siblings: how to weave unscathed through these myriad and rapidly changing emotional climates.

These subtle maneuvers had as their basis the granting of great latitude to others, both in attitude and behaviour, while at the same time remaining alert to the necessity of when (and how) to stand pat and cut the slack. That line between being manipulated (benign) and being co-erced (pernicious), though very thin was nevertheless quite discernible to her. The hair actually rose on the back of her neck at the latter. All in all, she convinced herself, it's enough to treat people decently and they will have no choice but to respond in kind.

So moving quickly, using money she had saved and borrowing a small amount from her mother (dismissing her mother's dismayed cry "But you don't know what it's like to live among uneducated people!" as incorrect—hadn't she grown up surrounded by them? forgetting the strong support the presence of her family had provided) she purchased a house and the fifteen acres surrounding it, paying cash, only making sure there was a suitable site for the passive solar house she planned to build. Indeed there was. A rise, southfacing, overlooking a pristine valley where cows grazed, with no other houses in sight.

The Director thanks the council for convening, reads the ordinance aloud, then says she believes the Baptist Church to be in violation of the ordinance. Silence. Several members exchange smug smiles.
Mr. Jenkins: Well, I think the bells are purty.
Director: I think that's irrelevant. We need to decide whether there is a violation.
Mr. Jenkins: You think it's what?
Director: Irrel..uh, doesn't pertain..uh, not on the subject.
Mr. Thornbuck: Well, they ain't very loud — you cain't even hear 'em where you live.
Director: I can assure you we hear them and they are loud.
Mr. Thornbuck: What?
Mrs. Frohm: Turn your hearing aid on, Joe.
Mr. Thornbuck: What?

Mayor: Well, Wilhelmine, we cain't do nothin about this, cause the ordinance says if any *person* creates a noise. The church ain't no person . . .

Director: Someone is responsible for turning the tape on. Mayor, are we in agreement that a violation does exist?

Mrs Ridgewell: Everybody but you likes the bells.

Director: I think that's irre..off the subject. The bells create a noise, noise is a violation of the ordinance. .

Mrs Ridgewell: I don't think its a noise.

Director: What would you do if someone played rock very loud downtown late at night?

Mrs Campbell: Well, that ain't the church.

Director: Precisely. So ...

Mrs. Ridgewell: Oh, I like all kinds of music—it wouldn't bother me.

Mrs. Campbell: Now we're all Baptists here and (leaning across the table) I don't know *what* you are.

Director: That's not the subject.

Mrs. Ridgewell: Oh, I don't know about that.

Mayor: Well, Wilhelmine, we cain't do nothin anyway. There ain't no law here. We cain't arrest nobody.

Director: I'm sure that's not necessary. If we can agree that a violation is occurring, a letter to the Pastor to that effect would be sufficient. I'm sure they don't want to break any laws, right?

Mayor: We just ain't got no authority to...

Director: You're the council, the ordinance is on the books, I think it's your responsibility to enforce ordinances. What do you do when someone doesn't pay their town taxes?

Mayor: Nothin.

Director: (laughs) Well, that's good to know ... Look, my primary reason for bringing this to your attention is because there is a law and laws shouldn't be broken with impun..uh, laws should not be broken. This violation affects my business, residents can't work because of the noise, and there wasn't any until the church installed this electronic carillon. My guarantee to the residents was that there would be quiet here. So if the ordinance isn't upheld I might have to close my business. Then the town will suffer because, I'll remind you, residents do buy from local merchants ...

Mayor: Well, Wilhelmine, wish there was something we could do but there ain't.

Director: I'd hoped we could resolve this issue without my taking further steps. But I do thank you for listening to me.

•   •   •   •

It was James' belief that by the time we reach adulthood, nearly all our behavior is automatic (habitual) from the time we rise from our beds in the morning until we retire at night. Dressing, undressing, eating, drinking—even our form of speech is so fixed by repetition as to be almost reflex action. So he maintained that habits are *had*, while his ardent admirer, Dewey, asserted that habits are *used*.

For Dewey, habits can only be understood in a biosocial setting i.e., as the effort to sustain coordination between a changing organism and a changing environment. As long as old habits are adequate for this, there will be no occasion for re-thinking; no occasion for re-thinking means no occasion for change. On the other hand, James believed we are richly endowed with instinctive reactions many of them universal (we smile when we're pleased) and that everything we do is restricted to those impulses, though throughout life they will continue to be modified, leading to behavior increasingly complex. Again, the interdependence of habit and learning. Further, he thought that the more details of daily life we can hand over to habit, then the more our higher powers will be set free for their proper work.

Interestingly enough, James was renowned for his spontaneousness, his restlessness and innovations, both in thought and behavior. Because of these qualities, it is said that his students were never bored. In Zen Buddhism we speak of "Zen mind, beginner's mind" as something to cultivate. And the practice of Zen is sometimes described as "doing what you are doing while you are doing it." Attention means attention.

•   •   •   •

February 18, 1986
ACLU, Southwest Chapter
Mr. Saul Ruark, Attorney at Law

Dear Mr. Ruark,

In reference to your letter (October 30, 1985), I have followed your suggestion with, unfortunately, no happy results. I spoke with a local attorney who refused to consider the case, no reason given. I contacted the St. Louis Volunteer Lawyers for the Arts only to discover after a long-delay that they handle only matters of tax-exempt status, copyright and lease agreements, etc. Finally I contacted another local attorney (Mr. Davidson, in Corinthia) who, though he was agreeable to writing the church officials, felt this approach would be ineffective and strongly urged me to re-contact you, as you suggested if I ran into problems. It was his feeling that since the church and town council have treated my own repeated requests with contempt, a letter from him would produce similiar results whereas that same letter from such a respected/feared source as the ACLU would have much better chance of success.

You have misunderstood my intention. I'm not seeking monetary reward (in form of damages, etc.) though the colony has been effected. Hence a contingency fee arrangement doesn't pertain.

I just want them to stop playing the damn bells!

I'd be most happy to come to Smithfield again and discuss further with you what can be done.

Sincerely,
Director, Neogaia Colony

March 18, 1986
Dear Ms. Bennett,

Will you please call and make an appointment the

week of 3/24/86. I am interested in pursuing your case on behalf of the ACLU.

Yours Truly,
Saul Ruark, Attorney at Law

<u>March 28, 1986</u>
ACLU, Southwest Chapter
Mr. Saul Ruark, Attorney at Law

Dear Mr. Ruark,

Here's the information you requested: the town of S. is incorporated.

The electric carillon was installed two years after Neogaia Colony opened.

The Mayor is Clint Stonefield. Members of the council are: (five names). Attached is a copy of Town Ordinance #17, regarding noise. Though I don't agree with you that broadcasting, against my wishes, Christian hymns into my living room repeatedly throughout the day *doesn't* constitute a violation of my right of freedom from religion, I'll be happy for you to use the right to Quiet Enjoyment to gain relief from this imposition. If, as you suggest, other members of the Chapter there might want to come and witness the bells, they begin at 9 AM and are played every half-hour after that, the last being at 7 PM, each rendition lasting about ten minutes. The church is located on Highway 7 just at the south edge of the village, but you will hear it long before you see it. Just follow your ears.

I am, of course, delighted that the ACLU is engaging themselves in this matter. If there is any way I can be of further assistance, don't hesitate to contact me. Regards.

<u>May 12, 1986</u>
Southwest Chapter, ACLU
Saul Ruark, Attorney at Law

Dear Mr. Ruark,

As you suggested, I contacted Mr. Davidson, the same attorney I'd spoken to before. On the basis of your statement of the "probability" of a letter issuing from the ACLU coincident with his, he did write and send the letter. Since your letter was *not* forthcoming, given the nature of these people, we have doubts that his letter will prove effective—but we've discussed this before. Indeed, the ACLU's failure to support this effort has placed me at risk. Shortly after the minister received the lawyer's letter I was accosted on the street by a member of his church (and my closest neighbor) and threatened that if I did not "call my lawyers off this", they would run me out of town. Mr. Davidson declined to accept the case on a contingency basis since he feels that only access to a federal court would insure an impartial jury.

And now I learn, via our phone conversation yesterday that the *reason* the ACLU is withdrawing is that the president of the chapter will not agree to the contemplated action because he is a minister! I am appalled.

Artists, be they painters, writers, composers, inevitably stand apart from the prevailing culture, this as a result of their own nature and because it affords them the necessary objective viewpoint. It also puts them at risk and the more closed the society, the greater the risk. They manage their vulnerability by a variety of means but sometimes these fail and they must seek protection elsewhere. I had always believed the philosophy of the ACLU was in alliance with this critical viewpoint, and shared the understanding of its necessity if a society was to remain viable. That belief has been badly shaken. While I recognize that, as a chapter, you are merely part of the whole, still, you are a representative of that whole so your actions must be considered as issuing from the whole. Yet your handling of my request for support, in a case I would have thought emminently suitable for ACLU involvement, was exemplified by indecisiveness, delays, implied support which never materialized, breech of faith, all of this producing almost as much stress as the situation for which I sought remedy. Shall I conclude then that in the circumstances I find myself, a lawless act is most effectively rebuffed by an equally lawless act?

I am keenly disappointed with your chapter's handling of my request for assistance.

Sincerely,

ACLU
132 West 43rd St.
New York, NY
June 26, 1986
(form postcard)

Dear Ms. Bennett:

We have received your recent request for assistance. Your request has been forwarded to: ACLU of Kansas and Western Missouri. In the future, please contact that office directly.

Sincerely,

(Over the printed address of the ACLU headquarters is stamped in red ink: DEFEND THE BILL OF RIGHTS SUPPORT THE ACLU)

August 15, 1986
ACLU of Kansas and Western Missouri

Dear Ms. Bennett,

I am sorry the ACLU of Kansas and Western Missouri will be unable to help you. As you know, the Southwestern Missouri Chapter has made a judgement about the involvement of the ACLU in this case and we support their decision.

Sincerely,

(Note: no official notice regarding judgement was ever received from the SW Chapter—only the communique by phone that the president would not agree because he was a minister.)

Because of the threat by the church member and more particularly because he was her neighbor and known for his violent behaviour, which included killing pets whose owners he was angry with, the director applied to the county sheriff for protection and/or advice. The sheriff's office sent her to the circuit court who sent her to the county prosecutor who sent her back to the court who sent her back to the sheriff. Full circle, she gave up.

· · · ·

Move up the evolutionary ladder to a more sophisticated nervous system and the responses to stimuli become less automatic, less predictable, more "intelligent", and their variety increases incalcuably. We share with other animals the ability to join sign and the thing signified: the cat hears the can opener and goes to stand by its bowl expectantly; we hear the bell and it signals (becomes) the Good Humor Man, the oven buzzer means the bread is finished baking. Obviously, such learning depends upon experience and when these are abundant the end result can be a kind of WISDOM. More often than not, though, we avoid adding anything new or foreign to our treasury of experiences and this poverty reduces the variety of available responses. Then too, when we do allow a new experience, we tend to accept it as an addition to, not replacement for, the old. This lack of reappraisal leads to a chaos of conflicting responses—a fibrillation of the organism. Now add to this that we tend to perceive only what we pre-perceive, and we pre-perceive mainly that for which we have labels (the experience fits the label, not vice-versa). And if our only labels are, say, "tree" and "witch" then everything is made to fit these labels. But the bell is not the Good Humor Man, not the ice-cream, the oven buzzer is not the bread. The Zen adage is to not mistake the finger pointing to the moon pointed at.

• • • •

"See, you can't tell the difference, can you?"
"It does taste like the real thing—what did you say was in them?"
Ray is still in the process of becoming a vegetarian.
"Lentils, bulgar, soy flour, onions, shoyu, uh ... I think thats all," recited the director.
Lisa, teasing, "Maybe you'd like to become sole cook for the next month?"

Ray, here for a residency of two months, has had bad luck with the concurrent residents. The first, a woman poet who vomited out her unfocussed and unmediated anger into her work, and because Ray was sweet and unassertive, he became the vessel into which she poured all her accumulated bile, seeking him out for this purpose any hour of the day or night.
He hadn't fared much better with the next one, a woman who appeared quite capable until it was her turn to prepare the meal or wash the dishes. Ray, perforce, had good-naturedly assumed these chores. She also managed to avoid any colony work during her residency. The colony being non-profit, fees were kept low ($65. per month) with residents expected to donate eight hours of work per week to the colony—either in the large garden which supplied their vegetables, or mowing the lawn, building a stone wall, whatever they chose. But now, the director is gratified to notice, Ray has lucked out for the three residents seem equally responsible and quite compatible.
"That full moon last night was too much for me. I slipped out about 2 AM—you know, living in the city you forget there are stars, moons ... "
"Only one." Ray introjects.
"It makes the world seem much larger," Lisa continues,
after punching Ray's shoulder. "I thought about gathering a few stars or moons to take back with me, a reminder. I could have, you know, they were in easy reach.

17

Anyway, I saw your lights on (to Ray) were you working that late?"

The director rolls her eyes. "Ray would work 24 hours a day if he could. In fact, I'm surprised he joined us for our picnic."

"Fourth of July? Independence Day? Don't you know how patriotic I am? How could I miss this celebration? But actually, I prefer working at night. It's sort of seamless, you know? No meals to interrupt and, ahem, NO CARILLON HYMNS!"

"Ha! You should have been here last summer —this is a tremendous improvement."

"Gee, what was it like then", Edwina asks.

"Ten minutes every half-hour and, you won't believe this, but even louder than it is now. It's true the tapes were in better shape you didn't get all the glissandi and flattened notes like someone is on a roller coaster and verrry nauseous. Though musically speaking, I think that might improve them. In fact, anything would improve them. I can't tell you how often I've thought of sneaking in and substituting,oh. say, something like Penderecki's Threnody —can you imagine their faces when that came blaring out?"

"Our luck, they probably wouldn't notice,"Edwina laughs.

"Some people from town told me—you know that racetrack outside of Lakeland?"

"The car racetrack?"

"Yeah. Early last spring they went there one evening before the races started and were sitting there when Lo, they heard bells—hymns wafting over them, and recognized the famous, or infamous, Baptist church carillon. That's twelve miles away! Anyway, now they only play it, like five times daily, sometimes more, it's erratic. But it's still less frequent and the volume is down some"

Lisa: "It's still an abomination. Did you have something to do with the change? And," she adds as the director pauses, "if so, can't you get them stopped completely? Isn't it against the law?"

"Yes to the first question, probably no to the second, and yes to the third. Now: shall we have our dessert—and then to the real fun, TA-DA! Fireworks!"

"Is it dark enough", Edwina worries.

Ray: "If we eat our dessert very slooo, it will be."

"Where do you get fireworks?" asks Lisa.

"No law against selling them here. I keep them on hand all the time because I like them. And because I celebrate so many things."

"I love celebrations."

Edwina teases, "Even when it takes you away from your work?"

"Listen. For Independence Day let me tell you..."

"You know what's fun? Creating traditions here at the colony. We've celebrated summer solstice, in a particular way, for the past three summers. And this is our second 4th of July picnic. None of the celebrations are—we don't have blueprints, it sorta gets re-created each time within a kind of framework with everybody contributing. But the fact of celebration is set. I'm not much of a traditionalist, but there's something very satisfying ..."

"I think it's because there's room for creativity each time. It doesn't get heavy with obligation either to what we did last year or to any particular person ...

Ray: "So that means you're really celebrating rather than blindly repeating a custom."

"Yeah, I think you're right. And if any of you want to initiate a tradition while you're here, just give the word ..."

"OOOOOOh, that was nice!"

"Now get ready for this one, it's called Lotus Secret Revealed. Wait a minute-which one do you have Ray?"

"Great Celestial Fountain."

"Oh my, let's do yours first."

"Well, that was a pretty piddley fountain. All right, Wilhelmine, reveal your lotus secret..."

"Oh!"

"Ooh, would you look at that!"

"Wonderful!"

"I liked that! Nothing spectacular, then that pregnant pause while you wonder if that's all and ..."

"... kinda like life, eh?"

"... and then all hell breaks loose and then even more,those subtle little blossoms floating out. . ."

"It *is* alot like life!"

They slowly gather the picnic things together then, pleasantly tired, walk home in silence.

"Jesus, would you look at that moon?"

"Yeah."

"Just one peaceful, beautiful day after another," murmurs the director.

Edwina: "I suppose that *could* get boring ... "

Ron, yawning. "Yeah, sure, after 10,000 years maybe..."

• • • •

See bear—feel frightened—run.

While we tend to think this the proper sequence of events, James' theory of impulsive (habitual) behaviour versus free agency is that we see the bear—run—feel afraid. As proof, he offers this: in pathological cases such as anxiety attacks wherein the emotions have no object, the "victim" begins hyperventilating, their heartbeat becomes erratic, they tend to take a crouching position and become immobile. Their stomach and sphincter muscles clench, all of this occurring automatically in this state of morbid fear. However, were the victim to gain control over his breathing, which in turn would regulate the heartbeat and relax the body, the fear would leave. So the emotion here is the expression of a bodily state. If I ask you to feel anger and you achieve this, it will be accompanied (or preceded) by the appropriate physical symptoms; if it is not it remains purely cognitive, a *perception* (see bear), an end in itself, lacking the dynamics of emotion.

On a return visit to New York after many years, years during which circumstances concerning safety had become quite complicated, I asked the friend I was visiting for advice. Later, I visited another friend down in the Village, stayed much longer than I had intended and

20

found myself in the subway, alone, at midnight. That is, alone until an African-American male appeared on the platform directly opposite me. It took a while for me to recognize that all of the components of the scenario my friend had warned against were present: alone, in the subway, late at night, with a male present. Oh, I thought, I should be frightened. Various antidotes rushed through my mind: I could run up the stairs onto the street where there must be other people. He could run up the stairs, run down the stairs to me... As I am trying to *instill* fear into my being which will enable me to act prudently, we are studying each other across the platform. I see nothing in him which will assist me in finding a reason for feeling fear. It is at this moment, looking straight at me, that he begins to whistle Bach. We smile, my train comes in, and to the accompaniment of *"Jesu, Joy of Man's Desiring"*, pulls out, my fear remaining mere concept.

• • • •

ITEM FROM DIRECTOR'S LOG:

July 10, 1986

G., my neighbor, comes along on his tractor, spraying my property. I run out and ask if he's spraying pesticide. He yells yes, I tell him I don't want my property sprayed. He aims the wand and sprays me, then continues spraying to the end of my property.

The director hurries to the resident's house where the garden is. The strange, not unpleasant smell of the pesticide is strong on the path through the woods but she can no longer smell it when she comes into the open garden area. She hesitates for a while then makes a decision, telling the residents there is a strong possibility the garden has been sprayed "by mistake" and for safety sake no vegetables should be used.

The next day she pulls up all the vegetables, puts them in garbage bags until she can think how to dispose of them. She feels certain that the neighbor, known for his temper, has made whatever point he wanted to make and will now be satisfied.

July 21, 1986
G. sprays my property again with pesticide, the wind being towards my house and garden at 8-10 miles per hour. I make formal complaint with the State Department of Agriculture, they send investigator who indicates that appearance of plants, foliage, suggest 2-4D but can't determine until reports on specimens come back from lab.

August 21, 1986
Using his tractor, G. piles large logs and brush across my driveway. I clear it so truck delivering wood can get in. Later G. puts it all back. Then, in his truck, he begins driving wildly in tight circles in the yard of the resident's house, barely missing one residents car, grinning and waving at the residents when they appear at the door. Terrified, the residents come get me and I reassure them as much as I'm able. G. continues these antics 9-10 times a day for the next several weeks. Though I pile brush, rocks, an old lawnmower across south access of yard several times, he simply drives over them with his truck which he handles like a tank.

August 25, 1986
The investigator from the Agriculture Department interviews G. to ascertain which pesticide he used, in what strength, and whether he has a license. Immediately after the investigator leaves, G. parks his truck in the residents lane, blocking their access or egress for almost three hours while he cuts down trees in my woods. I tell him he is trespassing and order him off my property, he merely starts shouting that he will run me out, make me sorry I ever came here. When he leaves, I put up NO TRESPASSING signs all over, he comes back and yanks them down. Using his truck, he knocks over the colony sign which is set in concrete.

August 28, 1986

At 7 AM G, on his tractor with the brushhog attached, starts mowing the area around the residents house, across the road from it, both sides of my access lane, then back to the house, zipping across the yard within inches of the resident's car, grinning, waving, acting crazy. Again they come to get me. He has mowed down all my fruit trees, bush cherries, blackberries, everything. Later he comes and mows around my house too.

August 30, 1986

The residents, too frightened to stay, have decided to leave early and I do not discourage them. I ask them to make written statements before they leave as to what they have witnessed. Now that they are gone I am free to confront G. if he continues.

Sept 1, 1986

See and hear G. telling Nate to bulldoze a section by my house and a corridor through my woods where he was cutting timber last week. Bettina, an acquaintance, is here and tells me I must not confront them but I do. While she stands safely in the yard I go up and tell them both they are trespassing and will be held liable for any damage done. G. goes wild, throwing his arms about, shouting that no one tells him what to do and that it's all his land anyway. I tell him to go to the assessor's office and find out who's paying the tax, he yells he doesn't have to, he knows what's his. Then he shoves me. I back away. He's very wild. As I leave he again yells he will make me sorry I ever came here, that he'll burn me out. Later I again put up NO TRESPASSING signs—and again he comes back and tears them down. I call his wife, ask her to reason with him and that if he sincerely believes some of this is his property he should check with the assessor's office. She is non-committal and seems to think it's of little importance despite my urgency. Later I find out that G. had already purchased a map from the assessor's office and is well aware of property boundaries. It seems just a ruse to give him a "legitimate" reason for his outrageous behaviour. I recognize that there is cunning here.

Sept. 2, 1986

At 7 AM G. comes with his chain-saw and begins to cut my trees. I go to call the sheriff and while I stand waiting for him Nate, the bulldoze operator, drives up in his truck. Again I tell him that if he does any damage he will be held responsible. He assures me he wants nothing more to do with G., everybody knows about him, he's just come to pick up his dozer. After a while G. stops cutting. It seems he's making some kind of corridor in my woods, and leaves before the deputy comes. When he does come, I tell him about the threats and harrassment, show him the damage from the brushhogging, tree-cutting, etc. I tell him I'm very frightened and even more afraid now that I've called the sheriff because I think G. will retaliate. He reassures me, pats me on the shoulder saying, "Well, nothing could be worse than it is now, could it?" He goes to see G.

Later, when I see him driving out, apparently not intending to stop, I run out to the road. He says that G. claims it's *his* land so he, the deputy, can't do anything. I tell him G. is lying and ask him to check with the assessor. He says no, it's a dispute between G. and me. Ask if I can't get protection and he suggests I see the county prosecutor. I call Bettina and we drive in to see the prosecutor but he's not in his office today so we go to the sheriff, tell him of the threats, trespass, property damage, show him the letters from the two residents which he reads carefully. Bettina has been urging me to get a gun for protection. She is also interested in the legalities of using a gun in circumstances where life is threatened. She asks the sheriff how I can protect myself. He says I should get a big club and hit him (G.) just below the kneecap (he demonstrates) saying you can do a lot of damage that way. Bettina asks if he doesn't think I should have a gun and he replies it would be a good idea. But she couldn't actually shoot him, could she? Bettina asks. Well, if he's on your property and coming at you yes, you can shoot him—try to hit him in the legs. This conversation is beyond my capacity to handle and to my embarrassment I begin to weep. The sheriff is sympathetic and asks if I'm willing to make a written statement describing incidents which have occurred. This I do while he makes copys of the resident's letters. I am not given a copy of my complaint. He then says he will make an inquiry. Feeling much relieved, Bettina and I go again to the assessor to ask how they determine property lines and they suggest we go to the abstract company which we do and where they tell us they will make a search of G.'s deeds to make sure there is no basis for his claims.

Sept. 4, 1986
Abstract company informs me G.'s claims on the property are not valid. I contact G.'s lawyer, explain the situation and he promises to tell G. to leave me alone. Also inform sheriff that abstract company found nothing to dispute property lines and are quite willing to talk to him about it if he wants to call them.

The purchase of land and house relieved a packet of worries for the director. Never again would she have to concern herself about noise issuing from adjoining apartments, too-close houses; never again have to admonish herself not to get attached to that tree lest the landlord decide to cut it down. Finally, a sense of security settled in and the energy bound up in all those anxieties were free to use constructively.

It was not until she was notified of her real-estate taxes that her dilemma confronted her. To pay taxes on property meant you "owned" it (an absurdity, she believed). Further, it meant she would be supporting such agencies as the local schools (reprehensible), the library (a joke), and health benefits (non-existent). In short, that luxury of living in accordance with her convictions, assured by her choice of voluntary simplicity and *not* being a property owner was now removed from the equation and she stood, painfully bi-sected by beliefs and actions which were contradictory.

She had, in effect, given up her freedom.

Then a transcendent experience, a stay at an artists colony, led her to her solution: start a colony. If she donated land and buildings for the purpose of a non-profit corporation she would be rescued from the obloquy of putting money (via property taxes) into institutions she considered noxious; the onus of ownership was removed and she became mere custodian, responsible to the land, trees, etc. The beauty she found here would be shared, for a purpose she found compelling. And, finally, because by this time she was missing terribly the graces of culture—she would simply import it. The first step then was to create housing for the director, and she hoped she would find others willing to alternate with her in this capacity, so that the existing house could serve the residents.

She began teaching herself how to build a house.

•   •   •   •

Any organism capable of response to stimulae must develop pathways of discharge. Associations of: ideas, perceptions, memories, etc. can best be understood as the formation of these neural paths (ruts) of discharge which are then used forever after unless consciously changed. Many of our actions have been co-opted i.e., taken over by habit to the extent that we must actually *perform* the act to know, say, which shoe we put on first. And in those habitual actions which consist of a particular chain of events, each link is precipitated by the muscular action of the preceding link. We might almost speak of muscular memory. Hence a dancer performs the first component of a movement and the other components follow automatically to complete the phrase.

Conversely, in a *voluntary* action, each link of the chain must be guided by idea and volition. In Jefferson's play, the drunken Rip Van Winkle excuses himself from each dereliction by saying, "I won't count this time. " Well, *he* may not, and others may not, but down among his nerve-cells and fibres it *is* being counted and stored to be used against him when the next temptation comes. In fact, nothing we do, in scientific literalness is *not* counted. Hence whatever habits we choose to establish in youth is to draw a portrait of ourselves in maturity.

• • • •

Sept 14, 1986
G. comes with the tiller on his tractor and tills my land where he previously brushhogged. And again he pulls logs and rocks across my driveway. He puts rolls of old fence across the lane to the residents house, knocks the colony sign down again which I had just re-set in concrete.

Sept. 15, 1986
Report the above incidents to the sheriff. He says he will have to issue a summons to G.

October 1, 1986
G. continues to drive across yard of the residents house. When I put rocks and brush there he simply drives over or around them. Because of excessive rain, he makes deep ruts all across the yard. I call his lawyer, he says he will talk to G. again. I have also consulted a lawyer, Davidson, who tells me I should record everything that happens immediately after it happens and take pictures of the damage. At first this seems silly, I keep thinking this terrible "mistake' will be righted any moment, that G. will come to his senses, or the sheriff will act as a sheriff should. But as the incidents pile up I see he gave me good advice.

• • • •

Though many different kinds of meditation exist, the practice and effects bear a strong resemblance to each other. Zazen or "sitting Zen" is not, strictly speaking, meditation, though it is a way of quieting the mind. An experiment was carried out to determine if qualitative differences existed between these various approaches. The subjects consisted of experienced

Transcendental Meditators, students of T.M. (who had been practicing only a couple of weeks), Yogi, and Zen Masters. All were instructed to meditate and brain waves were recorded for each. All quickly produced alpha rhythm, including the students, the only difference being that the Yogi and Zen Masters produced alpha of more amplitude. A loud noise was introduced. All meditators lost their alpha then quickly regained it. Another loud noise, and again alpha was lost. But very soon habituation occurred and even though the noises became louder and lasted longer, the meditators maintained their alpha rhythm through it. That is, all except the Zen Masters, who lost their alpha each time the noise occurred.

For them, each time was the first time.

· · · ·

October 9, 1986

G. still driving across the yard. Go back to sheriff who says G. is either crazy and should be in a hospital or mean as hell and should be in jail. I say nothing but don't think he's crazy except when he's in a rage. Then he is certainly psychotic with little or no control. I've seen these rages and heard others speak of them.

January 3, 1987

G. is cutting trees again on my property—this time near my house rather than the residents. It's not merely the waste—usually he cuts and leaves them where they fall—but the responsibility I feel as steward to protect these trees. Instead, because of me, they're being cut just for spite. Bettina is here while he's cutting. We simply stand and watch, at a safe distance. I don't try to talk to him any more because he just turns off his hearing aid and starts yelling at me. After he finishes, he pulls more logs across my driveway, yells at me that I'm a "trouble-maker", and shouts back as he gets into his truck to leave, "nobody tells James G. what to do!"
I report the cutting of trees to the sheriff.

<u>January 5, 1987</u>
He comes back and begins to cut the logs into firewood.
Bettina is here, but again we don't say anything, just bear
silent witness. The silence seems to bother him. He says to
me, "Do you know why I do these things? It's because you
don't love my Jesus. And I'll keep on doing them until you
get down on your knees and pray with me." My lack of
visible response seems to incense him further and he starts
yelling, "You want me to pray for you, trouble-maker? I'll
pray for you!"
He gets down on his knees in the field and asks God to save
"this trouble-maker." Then he gets up and resumes cutting
my trees.
He piles brush near my driveway, adding to the brush he's
already put there and says he will come back and burn the
brush, burn me out. He gets in his truck and leaves.

• • • •

In *Varieties Of Religious Experience,* James admits there is
no way to distinguish the religious from the neurotic. Nor
does he rule out the violently psychotic as being genuinely
religious. In fact, he was not so much attempting to define
religion as he was the religious life—which to him
consisted of the belief that there is an unseen order, and
that our supreme good lies in harmonious adjustment with
it. Examples he cited ranged from mere intuition, to
hearing voices and seeing visions, because these
experiences could be either useful or harmful depending
on their effect on the person's life. Thus the validity of the
religious experience depended on its *pragmatic* value: does
it work? what are the results?

• • • •

<u>January 6, 1987</u>
G. is back, saying he will burn the brush he's been
stacking near my woods. The wind today is 25-30

miles towards my house and woods. Contact Conservation Department, they say they'll keep watch from a helicopter and tell me to also alert village Volunteer Fire Department. Bettina comes and we spend the day clearing leaves and brush from around all buildings.

January 7, 1987
G. comes about 7 AM, pours gasoline on the brush he stacked, fires it and leaves in his truck. I call Conservation Department and village fire department. There is not much wind today. The fire department keeps control of fire which burns most of the day. Just before dark, I douse the rest of the coals but G. comes back, finds more brush and starts it up again. After he leaves, I again douse it and keep watch most of the night.

January 8, 1987
Notify sheriff's office about fire, filling out yet another complaint form which seems a futile effort. Later G. comes with his tractor and pulls a telephone pole across my driveway. There is no way I can roll that out of the way but for some time now I've been parking down at the residents house and walking back because I was so tired of clearing my drive each time.

•   •   •   •

Dewey's assertion that habits are used to maintain coordination between changing organism and changing environment can apply, for instance, in the case of a recent widow who continues the habit of going to concerts every second Tuesday, even though she doesn't particularly enjoy them, simply because this was an activity she shared with her husband. However there is no utility in the habit of persisting in preparing meals for two when she is the sole diner. For this is now triggered by denial and is cause for concern. It is as though one part of the mind operates in secrecy, incummunicado with other, monitoring, aspects of the mind. This splitting off, whether it be of action, thought, or emotions is, of course, typical of schizophrenia. However, when used in Dewey's adaptive manner, with some deliberation and on a temporary basis, it may have value.

Then how to make the distinction between hypocrisy and/or cunning and the above device of dissociation? In dissociation, the split is *within* the mind and though it may have been achieved by conscious effort, it depends upon that awareness being withdrawn for its continued existence. In cunning and hypocrisy there may be deliberation but the split exists between the "false front" and the "behind the scenes". Hypocrisy, practiced on occasion by almost everyone, can become such a habit, its use so skillful, that deliberation is no longer involved and no split discernible either to the user or others. Its effect is deadly. Cunning, on the other hand, is always purposeful and ambitious. Hence it is not a habit—though the tendency to use it can be a habit. Cunning, perhaps simply intelligence gone awry, can be used to great advantage. Particularly against the innocent.

•   •   •   •

February 3, 1987
Very early in the AM, hear a chain-saw up near the residents house. Hidden in the woods, I watch G, sawing limbs off trees, cutting small cedars near the house. He has taken to doing these small, rather inconsequential acts, more for their annoyance value and to keep me in a constant state of tension. I return home, then later, when the sound of the chain-saw is renewed, go back to discover he has pulled his truck onto my property and is now cutting down a large oak, one I happen to be particularly fond of because of its unusual oriental-shaped limbs. Lest he be startled and cut himself, I walk around in front of the truck before I confront him, yelling he should get off my property. He immediately starts yelling back, then he walks steadily towards me with the saw still running. I back away, he turns off the saw and throws it into the truck-bed but grabs a splitting maul and comes after me as I run down the road home, yelling all the way that he'll get me, he'll get me. Drive to sheriff, tell a deputy what happened and make a

31

written statement. This time I insist on a copy. He tells me to go to the prosecutor, tell him about all the incidents including this one and that the sheriff's office will provide him with their reports. I tell him I'm afraid to return home, that G was still on my property when I left, I ask for protection. He says they'll get on this right away, pull G. in for assault with a deadly weapon. The prosecutor is not in today or tomorrow so I make an appointment for the following day. I am afraid to return home but recognize I must.

•   •   •   •

It is the prey's movement which attracts the predator. So-called "shamming death" is not that at all but rather paralysis because of fear. Humans somewhat modify this by holding their breath, remaining immobile. Even impressions too faint and delicate to be detected are immediately known if they move: Fly sitting is unperceived, moving down your arm, its presence is instantly recognized.

✪   ✪

I take my evening walks on these country roads much later now. Before, it was my way of saying good-night to the moon, stars and sky before going to bed. Now I feel safer, if I go out at all, at two or three AM when nobody is abroad. I avoid roads where there are houses with dogs—lest they bark and alert someone.

February 5, 1987
See prosecutor. Tell him of the systematic harrassment, threats, trespass and property damage for the past eight months and, finally, the assault two days ago. He folds his hands and says that this is a civil matter and he will not get involved. I say, through my astonishment, that surely at least the assault is a criminal action. He says, well, he didn't

actually hit you, did he? I tell him what my understanding of assault is in legal terms but he simply repeats that he will do nothing. You should get a lawyer, he says. I tell him I can't afford to retain a lawyer nor do I think it appropriate. That when a criminal act has taken place law officials should act. He shrugs. You can sign a complaint form and talk to my investigator, that's all I'll do, he says and quickly ushers me out, tells his secretary to have me sign a complaint form. I sign a blank form, thinking I suppose, that I will then be expected to fill it out myself.

Then the investigator comes but will not allow me to talk about anything except the assault. Each time I try to mention the fire, threats, tree-cutting to show how things have escalated, he stops me. He, himself, fills out the complaint form which I have already signed. When I ask, he says G. will be picked up. I ask if that will be today, he says probably not until tomorrow.

February 8, 1987
The sheriff comes out (while G. is in church) and looks over my land. I show him where the tree was felled (at time of assault), where G. has cut other trees, where the fire was, point out telephone pole still blocking my drive, where brushhogging was done, fruit trees mowed down, relating these events to my survey map as we walk around. Gazing at all this destruction afresh, it looks like some terrible disaster has struck—or like a war zone. The sheriff says he can't figure out why G. does these things. I remind him of what G. said ("you don't love my Jesus"). He asks if we've had quarrels about religion. I tell him that when I first moved here G. would frequently ask me to attend his church and I would simply thank him for the invitation then not go. When G. persisted, I finally told him I had my own religion. The sheriff asks (fishing) if I told G. what that was. I say no, I consider religion to be a private matter. He takes pictures of the damage and leaves before G. returns.
I feel very hopeful. It seems that finally the destruction can be stopped.

33

<u>February 10, 1987</u>
G. still not picked up. He comes and brushhoggs again even though there is nothing to mow down anymore.

❂   ❂

There is a small group of homesteaders, all auslanders like the director, who live some distance away. They repeatedly point out to her that obviously the sheriff will do nothing to protect her or her property, that G. and others in the community, those who plague her at night by pulling into her drive (as far as the telephone pole) and yelling, "Come out witch!" become more incensed when she reports to the sheriff. They insist that she must get a gun for protection. Everything in her revolts against this. Try as she might she has never been able to make the association of gun with protection. At the age of seventeen, home from her first year of college for the Christmas vacation, her twenty-three year old brother, by accident or suicide, had shot himself. She was the first in the family to run to him in the next room. Forever after, Christmas meant horror, and guns, even the sight of them, meant death. Yet at the same time she feels she has no right to seek the homesteaders support unless she is willing to take their advice.

❂   ❂

<u>February 11, 1987</u>
I go to the sheriff's office and sign a permit to purchase a gun. A 36-hour waiting period is required. Today, G. cuts limbs, small trees. Now he does this when my car is gone, leaving the carcasses where I'm sure to see them. I think his purpose is to suggest that during my absences he can do anything. Which of course he can. Bettina tells me that concern for my safety led her to call the prosecutor and ask that I be given protection. He got angry and repeated that he wasn't going to do anything about this matter, that I'd just have to "shell out" for a lawyer. She asked, pointedly, if

34

there was some official she and concerned others could write to, and he said she could write anyone she damned pleased and hung up. I call sheriff to find out why G. hasn't been picked up. But the sheriff is out of town. I leave a message for him to call me. He doesn't.

February 12, 1987
Go to see Davidson, the attorney I've consulted periodically. He tells me that prosecutor has full discretionary powers, he can call an apple an orange, an assault a civil action if he chooses. Without irony, he tells me this is for citizen's protection because it places the prosecutor beyond influence. However, he does call the Assistant Prosecutor ("he owes me one") and says: "Jack's (prosecutor) at it again!". So I see this assistant prosecutor, tell him of the assault, he promises to talk to "Jack" but is not hopeful he will change his mind.

February 14, 1987
Thirty-six hours having expired, go to pick up gun permit but sheriff has not signed it. Am told he's out of town and return date is not known.

February 18, 1987
G. still not picked up. Write letter to a woman in his church congregation whom I know, (neighbor on the other side of me) essentially an open letter to the congregation, setting forth what has happened, asking that they speak with G.

February 21, 1987
Sheriff has finally signed gun permit (the 36 hours stretched to 10 days). Ask advice of Walmart clerk about what to buy. When I pick one he says now I need to tell you that if you're getting it for protection this won't kill anybody, you'd need to get a bigger calibre for that. I tell him the smaller one is exactly what I want. Put the box in the back of my closet without opening it. Am very conscious of it being there.

When she first arrived in the village the director had discovered that the main venue for communication was the post office. More precisely the post office from 8:30 to 9:30 in the morning during the wait for the mail to be distributed. This was when, and where, the villagers gathered and community news was exchanged. So for the first six months she delayed putting up a mailbox on her road, appearing each morning at the post office to allow the villagers to see who she was and to get some sense of who they were in addition to collecting the news.

Actually, the director was mistaken in this assumption. For the real news, that which might have important consequences for her, was dispersed in the churches, safely, among the congregation. Whether information was of general import (the water supply would be turned off on Friday) or private (don't tell, but it's the Corvil boys who are battering all the mailboxes—look out for them) you remained ignorant unless you made yourself a part of that congregation. And the real sense of who these people were could only be gained within those hallowed walls. If at all. For what the director will learn, too late, is that the smiling faces and friendly greetings are merely the faces they wear—not the people they are.

❂   ❂

I used to walk these country roads, freely and joyously, night or day, each familiar landscape seen as though for the first time. I still walk, but warily, glancing over my shoulder lest car, truck or pedestrian come upon me unawares.

❂   ❂

In the interest of protecting the organism from threatening changes in its environment, new habits can be installed. For instance, during stress, particularly prolonged stress, a habit of dissociating oneself from the stressing agent (denial) or even from the stressed self, can be utilized. This latter is accomplished by thinking and

36

referring to oneself in the third person, (Think of the tragedy of Mohammed Ali, who created a public persona, stepped into it, then discovered he could not get out).

There is another protective device associated with long-term stress, often achieved unwittingly. This is disorientation. More commonly this pertains to time rather than place, the person either entirely unable, or requiring clues, to fix themselves in the present. Time becomes a warped and flexible sculpture, events fall loose from their place, the sequence of events become garbled.

• • • •

February 24, 1987

G., using truck and trailer, brings seventeen bales, the large, round kind weighing 1000-1500 pounds each, and distributes them in the yard of the residents house, then places two across my drive next to the telephone pole. It is such an overdetermined, creative, outrageous act that a part of me wants to applaud his audacity. But when I stand next to these leviathan abominations I see how they dwarf not only the house and yard but myself as well. Because they are so large he can carry only three at a time. While he is going after yet another load, my rage boils over and I focus on his tractor which he has parked in my yard. Using a sledge-hammer and nails I pound and pound until I can puncture his tractor tire. As the air is released, squealing and hissing, so too is my anger released. Replaced by fear. This is my first retaliative act and though I've had strong hints that this is precisely what he wants, indeed that this is the only language this community understands and accepts, my fear escalates and I quickly return home and lock myself inside. Later, though, when he drives his tilted, loping tractor by, I smile broadly.

February 26, 1987

Sheriff comes out, tries to arbitrate with G. and myself, the three of us standing in the road in front of my house. G., after avowing he's never told a lie in his life, raises his arm in oath, "stack of Bibles", and says that he has been a good neighbor to me, never done me no harm. He claims to have finally found his deed proving the property his, and produces it. I point out that the deed pertains to the Northwestern Quarter (wherein lies his property) not the Northeastern Quarter (wherein lies mine). But the sheriff looks confused. I remind him that people in the abstract office, experts in such matters, have expressed willingness to talk to him at any time. Tell him that since G. will not accept the word of the assessor, his lawyer, the abstract company, I have ordered another survey of my property and suggest we treat the land he questions (though G. keeps changing the location and extent of this) as No Man's Land, neither of us using it until the survey is finished. G. will not agree to this.

March 7, 1987
Emboldened when G. doesn't directly retaliate for puncturing his tire, the director types a legal sounding letter warning him that if he doesn't remove the hay from her property by next Saturday she will not be responsible for it. Emboldened, yes. But she notices that she's so conditioned that even when he is not doing anything she is as apprehensive, perhaps more so, than when he is. At least when he is active she knows where he is, the extent and nature of the harm.

During the grace period, she calls the homesteaders, all of whom maintain large gardens and tells them about the hay. Since it is old and disintegrating, it will make excellent mulch and compost. By Sunday G. has removed none of the hay so, as planned, fifteen homesteaders come while he is in church and roll, with great and combined effort, the bales up planks into pickup trucks. With only three trucks, several trips are needed. The telephone pole blocking her drive is cut into movable sections and the two bales removed. One of the bales is held back in order to roll it down the sloping road, disintegrating all the way so that G. must drive through clumps of it.

On his return from church, as G. passes the resident's house, we are prepared. The women rush into the yard,

38

flamboyantly flexing their muscles to suggest that it was they and they alone who moved the one ton bales, all seventeen of them.

There is another item on the agenda for this day. The homesteaders have cheered the purchase of the gun and will instruct the director how to fire it. The first time she fires it, she collapses in sobs, memories rushing in. Embarrassed at her reaction, she resolutely fires again. And again.But after the homesteaders leave and she is alone to bear the brunt of how G. might react, again alone to accept the consequences of their "fun", she carefully, at arms length, removes the remaining bullets from the gun, then returns it to its pristine white box in the back of the closet.

❂   ❂

I walk the roads, secretly, as it were. I keep watch and bear witness to the destruction, seeing it both by daylight and moonlight. I seem to be functioning in a more or less healthy manner. My legs move. My hand writes. I prepare meals and eat them. And at night when I place my body on the bed it levitates with rage.

The director decides to go away for a month. Spends several weeks at a Zen Center on the coast north of San Francisco, then a week with her niece in Santa Cruz. At the Zen center, she frequently bursts into tears. Despite the concern of one of the monks, she is reluctant to talk of the cause of her emotionalism; her neice, having knowledge of the situation, inquires politely about it in a way which prohibits more than a casual response. She returns home in mid-April to find her driveway again blocked with logs. And decides to suspend operation of the colony this summer since she can no longer promise quiet or even physical safety to residents.

✪   ✪

As usual, after I've been away a while, I check the town cemetery across from the residents house hoping to find a new grave: G's. Since I found new logs in my drive I'm not hopeful but I do look. And find not G's, but Gus' grave, the mound of funeral flowers not yet wilted. Gus was my neighbor on the other side and as different from G. as it is possible to be. He was also, as far as I know, my only real friend in the community. He had been mayor for many years and, I gather, respected but not liked because he kept trying to introduce "newfangled ideas" (like a town sewer system!) . He also had a tendency towards honesty, not prized in this community.

I came to know him my first summer because of a leaking roof. So far I'd managed (had no choice really) to do all the needed repairs on my house but the width of the roof required a full roll of roofing and I didn't think I could carry 90 pounds up a ladder without a helper. The postmaster had referred me to a man, but after a couple of months of negotiating, which required my driving to his house (he had no phone) each time he didn't show up as promised, being greeted by his dozen or so dogs in various stages of disease and starvation, too weak to be a threat, and by the man's toothless, tobacco -stained mouth, reiterating his joke: no need to roof today, the suns shining, or its twin: can't roof tomorrow, it's gonna rain. Stereotypes do exist, I thought and stopped at Gus' house to ask if he knew anybody.

He and I had already spent afternoons on his porch, telling funny stories to each other, mostly about old cars and the mishaps we'd had with them. We got along splendidly, both very much at ease but when his wife, Mildred, joined us on the porch, that ease tightened some. She was religious in extreme and her notion of funny was to recite something she'd just read in GRIT, a religious magazine of the far right which, when I saw a copy years later, cleverly matches its title. All the same, she was the only one who showed interest when news that I would establish the colony appeared in the papers. "I'll feel too shy to talk to them because they're so educated", she said, but then, on reflection, added, "but you have a PhD and I don't feel shy with you."

After I asked if he could recommend anybody, Gus thought for a while before saying,"Nope." He thought a while longer then, "I'll do it."

I hesitated. Gus is 73, skinny, almost gaunt, and obviously not in good health though I don't know the nature of his illness. "Uh, well, Gus, that part of the house needing roofing is almost flat, but I wanted to do the garage too and it's pretty steep."

"Huh! I've worked on roofs a lot steeper than that!"

I saw that he needed to do this, needed to prove something, so I told him what I could pay. He snorted, "Never made that much an hour in my life!"

With his, "I'll be there at 7 AM", I went home to scrape off the two layers of roofing and myriad layers of tar which, because of the heat, had melded into a mass and had to be pried up inch by inch. Knowing that the hardest part of the job was done eased my worry about Gus. At 7 AM he was there with Mildred, who sat on a stump in the shade watching us work. Things went well, and in several halfdays (Glen left at 11:00 to avoid the heat) we finished the house with only a few good-natured arguments on the proper way to proceed.

We started on the garage which needed some of the decking replaced. Glen, much more competent with the power saw than I, cut out the rotten sections, calling down measurements while I sawed the replacement pieces. Again, some arguments, which we both enjoyed—he adamant, me caring less, so conceding. Then, after coming down the ladder for a break, he fainted. Mildred remained unruffled while I checked his pulse, elevated his legs, put cool cloths on his forehead, feeling stupid and inadequate. "Has he done this before?" "Never," she replies, yet continues to sit some distance away. Gus recovers, I insist he go inside where it's cooler and lie on my bed. He rests there a while then I drive them home in their car since his wife can't drive. His parting words are: See you in the morning.

41

The next day dawns as hot as the previous days so I pretend to succumb every 20 minutes or so, insisting we get off the roof and take a break. And this is the regimen we follow until the roof is finished. When I pay Gus, his delight and pride makes me turn away to hide tears.

The next summer, when I am building my house, sweating away 10 or 12 hours a day, sometimes I see a figure moving very slowly towards me across the meadow and I know it's Gus before I see the cane because he is the only one who is interested in what I'm doing. I feel both delight and concern—invariably he will sit only a while before he's working with me and he seems even more frail than the previous summer. Besides, he's mischievous. Once, as I am adding water carefully, because my tendency is to add too much, to a wheelbarrow of cement, he keeps yelling from his perch on a nearby concrete block, more! more! then comes over and dumps a whole bucket of water in, leaving me mortar with the consistency of ... well, water.

•   •   •   •   •

Another experiment, this one to determine if there is a qualitative/quantitative difference in response when the Rorschach is administered to subjects from the general public, Zen students, and Zen Masters. Without exception, the Zen students produced a greater number of original responses, often ten times the average of the general population. The Zen Masters saw ink blots. Only ink blots.

The advent of the Viet Nam War and the returning veterans brought a new disease entity, or more accurately, a new label for an old condition. Called Shellshock in World War 1, now it became Post Traumatic Stress Disorder, PTSD. Here, quite clearly displayed, is the habit of joining signal and thing signalled. But whereas before, the equation Good Humor bell=ice cream was appropriate, now imposed on the cue is a mis-response. Hence, at the sound of a car backfiring, the veteran may jump for cover under his bed or grab his rifle and run into the street to meet the danger. If, as Dewey maintained, the habit is flexible enough, learning will take place and behaviour will be modified so that response-to-signal is appropriate. However, if the psyche remains overwhelmed, habit becomes rigidified and unyielding. And because the originating traumatic or potentially traumatic stimulae had multiple associates, virtually anything—a smell, a sound, a certain visual configuration, can trigger this mis-response. Further, and even more devastating, is the fact that conditioning has taken place so that the threat has become ever present.

Habitual too, are recurrent nightmares which plague some returning veterans or, indeed, anyone who has undergone prolonged stress. These tend to have repetitive (habitual) content and the response (terror) is habitual as well.

How, you ask, is this different from Zen-mind-beginner's-mind which insists that each time an event occurs it is occurring for the first time? Thereby abjuring habituation? But event occurring-first-time must have, in the beginner's mind, a corresponding newness of reaction. Is an ink blot an ink blot?

• • • •

April 8, 1987
Legal Aid, Springfield, MO

Dear Legal Aid applicant:

Because of limited Legal Services Corporation and/or Older Americans Title 111-B funding to Legal Aid of southwest Missouri, only certain types of cases are presently being accepted for assistance.

(x) Child and spouse abuse

Even though Legal Aid has not accepted your application for assistance, this does not mean your case does not have merit. You may consult a private attorney, at your cost, if you wish to pursue this matter further.

43

May 18, 1987
People for the American Way

Dear Ms. Bennett,

I am shocked and saddened to hear of your troubles with your neighbors, community, the law officers, and the ACLU. To date, People for the American Way has assisted local school boards in two federal cases, the Mobile "secular humanism" trial, and the Church Hill "Scopes 11" trial. Our legal affairs department consists of three lawyers and one of these is a part-time employee. Due to our limited resources and the nature of our work, PEOPLE FOR cannot offer you legal representation in either the criminal or civil aspects of a case such as yours.

I am surprised that the ACLU turned you down and remarked that their president is a minister as if that were a reason not to help you. I would suggest you write directly to the minister and explain that you were denied assistance because it was felt he would not approve. I would also say that as a minister I am sure he would not condone such harrassment nor would he want to deny you the services of the ACLU. Depending upon his response would determine your next step. If the minister's letter is not to your liking, I would send copies of both your letter and his response to the ACLU national headquarters. If none of the above works, I would start a letter-writing campaign to the editor of your local paper and recruit the residents of your Colony to do the same. Once again, I am sorry PEOPLE FOR cannot be of more assistance. Please keep me posted. Sincerely,

<u>April-May 1987</u>

Appeals to various organizations, spawned in the 60's and 70's to protect civil rights, revealed that most were defunct. Appeal to the American Atheist organization, despite their claims to be ready to help those in my situation, elicited no reply. Numerous letters to editors of local papers, the Springfield Leader, St. Louis Post-Dispatch, throughout 1987, often tied in with an editorial, were not printed. The director later learns that a member of the editorial staff of the local paper is related to the sheriff.

June 5, 1987
Survey finally completed, boundaries essentially agreeing with assessors. Surveyor was aware of difficulties so markers were referenced (in case they were pulled up, reference would indicate their position). The marker in the field where G. had already annexed and fenced off a portion of the director's land was driven all the way in to escape detection.

July, 1987
One survey marker has disappeared.

August, 1987
The survey marker in the field has been dug up and taken.

• • • •

Shared habits, whether they be bowling every Saturday afternoon with a team of fellow workers, running three miles with Jody every morning at 6:30, alternating Sunday suppers with a group of women—all these can be powerful bonding agents. And often these shared actvities create a consensus of assumptions which may lead to shared conclusions. A husband and wife who share, for instance, the habit of hating and fearing dogs, all dogs, on sight, find this commonality a comfort. That which before had the possibility of being considered an irrational response to stimuli, is now relieved of the necessity of review and is instead reinforced. Hate/fear becomes the proper, the only, response to dogs.

Where such concurrences exist, we may now describe it as a conspiracy, i.e., habitual ways of thinking about or responding to one's environment which lead to attitudes or biases shared among a few or many. Even though these may remain unspoken the result of this sharing is a de facto act of conspiracy whether it occurs in a family or community. And where this tacit agreement is the

45

operant principle, those so bound together will act in concert. Therefore we can say that the test of whether or not a conspiracy exists is determined by the resultant appearance of collective action. Think of a mob lynching. And we may further assert that those gathering places where habits of conspiracy are fostered and practiced, whether they be schools, political halls, clubs, smoke-filled rooms, or churches—these can be deemed dens of iniquity.

•   •   •   •

The director makes plans to go away for two months to another artists colony in order to work. Working at home has been impossible because of the number of times each day, sometimes as much as twenty, G. passes and she has to leave her desk, walk through the woods to the residents house to make sure he has not destroyed, is not destroying, something. During the winter when the foliage is off the trees, she merely has to go into her yard for the extent of her property to be in view.

Fully conditioned now, it no longer matters whether incidents occur daily, weekly or monthly. Continued alertness has become a necessary obcession.

She leaves in September and returns in November, greatly redeemed. For she has been able to work diligently and, perhaps more importantly, contact with others has assured her that she could give and inspire warmth, and that earned respect, even esteem, was still possible.

"It was wonderful! You wouldn't know it was part of the US except they speak English..."

"It must have been good—you're glowing!" Vivien is the new town librarian. "I want to hear all about it. But listen, uh..."

Vivien looks away, opens and shuts a desk drawer then, still looking away, "Uh, do you mind if kids are in your house while you're gone?"

The director is puzzled. "You mean Sheila? She comes in to

feed my cats while I'm gone. I've asked her not to tell anyone when I'm away and not to bring any of her friends in with her so I'm sure she wouldn't." Vivien leans forward, so upset she spits out her words. "Listen, the next time you go away don't tell *anyone,* lock everything up and take your cats with you!" "Vivien, what do you know you're not telling me?" Vivien hesitates then reaches into her purse, brings out a paper and hands it to the director who also hesitates, then takes and reads it. It is a copy of the October issue of the local school newspaper, open to a page from which she reads:

> Has anyone heard of Wilamene?
>
> If you dare, there is a spookhouse, down
> a gravel road, across from the
> graveyard go to it.
>
> If you dare, have a look.
>
> There is a pit. Get a scare.
>
> If you dare, go inside, there is a
> chant, an odor of death.
>
> Run with fear, over the back fence
>
> Down the gravel road, back home.
>
> There is a witch, down a gravel road,across
>
> from the graveyard. Go there-IF YOU DARE!

"Who, what..." the director can hardly speak.
Vivien looks away.
"...and the kids in my house?"
"I don't know anything! And don't you dare mention my name with this!"
The director is stunned. Alone, and aware of it through all that's happened, she has been grateful to those who were truly supportive presuming, and respecting their wish that this support be kept private since they didn't indicate it be made public. But none had actually voiced this, trusting her, and none had made it clear they were

withholding information which might be vital to her.

"But Vivien, I've stood with you through so many of your troubles," the director reminds her, puzzled. "You're not to mention my name, do you understand?" Vivien is shouting.

She walks home trying to make a plan of action for obviously that's what is called for. And it must be quick and decisive. Otherwise she will be in grave danger. More danger than before. For the "poem" was an open invitation to the whole community. To carry out some action, some plan which heretofore might have been vague and amorphous. Well, she had learned this much: direct confrontation demanding someone be accountable for their actions only angered them further. But she sensed it also put a check, albeit temporarily, on their acting out their anger. When she retreated, on the other hand, it was like a wounded animal inviting them in for the kill.

What they intended was that she cower—as a woman should. That obeisance might serve as an apology for being the free person she was. If she convinced them that she was, indeed, "broken". would they lose interest? Certainly the homesteaders guessed correctly that the villagers were highly insulted when she sought remedy via law officials rather than, say, burning down their barn, shooting at them, or beating them up. These were "honorable" reprisals. For what they engaged in were feuds, wars which were insular, incestous, with, indeed, sexual overtones. And to parley with an outsider as she had done was tantamount to sexual betrayal.

Offensive to them too, was that she had performed kindnesses for some of the villagers when the occasion arose. Even, she remembers with a start, for G. himself before he started his campaign. This infuriated them because, having labeled her a witch she had, by god, better act like a witch. Building her own house, running or walking on the roads—in their eyes these were activities unsuitable for a woman. But her greatest crime, unspoken, was that she neither sought nor needed their approval. This was the source of their overwhelming frustration for how were they to bring her to her knees without this powerful weapon? Slippery, seemingly untouchable, she eluded them. And their rage grew.

Heretofore when some act had been committed against her, she had felt it important to make a conspicious appearance in the village, walking slowly and deliberately, eyes straight ahead, from the post office at one end of Main street to the other end and back. She felt exposed and vulnerable but instinct told her it was necessary, not as defiance but as reassurance to them (you haven't destroyed me) and affirmation of herself. It seemed too that she must keep undeniable reality in front of them lest their fantasies, which seemed inevitably violent, be allowed to run unchecked.

The next morning she goes to the school, walking past the secretary and directly into the Principals office, slaps the article onto his desk, demands: What is this? Do you know what libel is?

She has re-infused her rage before coming, knowing from experience that, untempered, it can carry her through this ordeal and any barriers they might erect. If she can keep the rage at the same pitch, she is invincible. The Principal, apparently with interest, reads the paper.
"I haven't seen this before."
She believes him but lest she lose her edge, reminds herself that this does not relieve him of responsibility.
"I want to see the student who wrote this and the teacher advisor for the paper! Here. Now." She slaps his desk for emphasis, gratified to think that probably at no time in his life has he seen a woman behave in this fashion.
"Oh. well..." he is shaken but still hoping some inspiration will come to grant him control. "I don't know which student, I, uh, the teacher, now she's new, she wouldn't know anything..."

49

"Here. Now."

The Principal speaks to the secretary. Soon the student appears in the doorway, too frightened to enter. The teacher pushes past the student into the room and sits. The Principal calls out their names as though in introduction, the director makes a point of writing them down.

She thrusts the newspaper into the student's hands.

"Read it. Aloud."

The student looks at the Principal, "Do I have to?"

"Yes!" hisses the director, leaning in towards her. She will make sure this experience is etched into the minds of these three. And begins, to a small degree, to enjoy herself.

The student, faltering, reads.

"Do you know me?" leaning close to the student.

"No, I..."

"Ever seen me before?"

"I don't know..."

"Then why would you write this dirty little..."

"I..I didn't..."

"Ah. Ah. Someone else, is that it? Or someone told you..."

"Someone told me what to say."

"And who was that?"

Almost whispering, to the Principal, "Do I have to tell her?"

"Yes!" the director hisses again, stands up and moves closer to the student. She is prepared, if necessary, to slap her. The student speaks two names.

The director sits abruptly, dazed. These are adults in the community. One is the grandson of the former librarian, the one with whom she had discussed Zen Buddhism years before with the stonings following hard upon. The librarian had pretended to be shocked by them and the director, confused, had forgotten that the librarian was the only one who knew she was a Zen Buddhist. And later, this same grandson, had come to her, telling of his concern because he had overheard others talking at school, *this* school, of plans to come that night and "really give her a hard time." He, and the kid who was with him, wanted her permission to frighten them so much they "would never bother her again."

And she had been touched by his earnest desire to protect her. In fact, it was he who had told her that the stonings were because she was a Zen Buddhist or witch. And thanking him, she had said she preferred to handle her own difficulties but might call on him in the future. It was that night that the new house had been broken into and she had not been able to find the grandson afterwards to ask whose conversation he had "overheard." He seemed to have dissappeared from the village.

Of course. All was a lie, the whole thing was a ruse and a well calculated one at that. He might also be involved in the night visitations since it was unlikely he would desist from mischief all these years then start again, unless his mind remained fixated.

The other adult named is also prominent in the community. Someone she has befriended on a couple of occasions and, she remembers with a jolt, the chief of the village fire department. Another frightening aspect is that, with these two, both of the other churches in the village become represented. So either the conspiracy has spread or had always been more broadly representative than she had guessed. She shivered involuntarily. There had been times in the months before she left when she had felt a malignant, ever-encroaching presence around her. Now she wonders if that was reality. For instance, the "poem' refers to a pit. Only someone who had been in her house would know there was a dropped area, a conversation pit around the woodstove. As for the chanting mentioned, she chanted a sutra after zazen. She feels defiled.

She turns to the teacher. "Now, Mrs. Baily."

"She's new on the staff, doesn't know the community,.." the Principal hastily intervenes.

Ignoring him, "Now, Mrs, Baily, when you see a vicious, scurrilous bit of tripe like this with a proper name attached, you don't get suspicious?"

"I didn't know it referred to a real person. Really."

"And no doubt in your experience the name Wilhelmine is such a common one that of course highschool students, particularly of the calibre we have here, would choose it."

51

"I really didn't think it was an actual person.

The director hesitates. "I believe you. Which means I accept your ignorance but," leaning closer to the teacher, "not your stupidity!"

The teacher winces.

"Are you learning anything from this?" inquires the director.

The teacher looks at her lap.

The director stands and addresses the Principal. "I have an appointment tomorrow with my lawyer. In the meantime, I will write a retraction and this will appear in the next issue of the newspaper. Further, when it is printed, you will instruct all of the students who were involved in this," she taps the paper on his desk," to handcarry a copy to my house and place it in my hands—understand?"

"I...I'll agree to the retraction but I'm not sure, I mean, I don't know whether I can get the kids to,.."

"You will *see* that they do. And that may mean that you come with them."

"Well, OK.

The director drives directly to the home of the editor of the paper whom she knows dates the librarian's grandson. It is the editor's sister whom she has just dealt with in the Principal's office. The mother, Mrs. Wheeler, answers the door, the director explains why she is there, shows her the paper. The director also tells her that her son has frequently driven by her house the past couple of years, at night, harrassing her.

"How do you know it was Chris?"

"I recognized his truck."

"Oh. Well, I don't always know where my children are or what they're doing—but why didn't you tell me about this before ?"

"You're right. I should have. But he'd harrass me for a few weeks—there were always other kids with him—and other cars for that matter, and I'd just decide to call you then he'd stop. I'd think, oh, good, he's come to his senses. Then a couple of months later he'd start again..."

"Well, he joined the army last week so he won't be bothering you anymore. But I do wish.,,"

She is interrupted by her husband who bursts into the room. Apparently Mr. Wheeler has been listening. He moves close to the director, his fist raised. "Now you listen to me! You come in here accusing my son, something you made up..."

"I know his truck."

He is shaking with rage, reminding her of G.

"Now, Don, just be calm..." his wife attempts.

"Everybody in this town has a truck like that!"

"I have the license number."

"You took it from his truck out in the drive," he shouts, moving even closer to her. He is a small man, his head bullet shaped with hair cut very close to the skull.

"Now I'm going to tell you something," he shouts, "you better change your lifestyle if you're going to live around here!"

"Now, Don.." his wife admonishes.

The director is puzzled. "Do you know me? Because I don't think I've ever seen you..."

"I don't have to know you," he is still shouting and shaking. The director would like to move back a few inches from him but does not think this wise.

"I've heard all about you," he continues, "and you'd better change or ... you had better change!"

The director, assuming a calm she does not feel, thanks the wife for listening and leaves.

Next she goes to see Andy, who still lives with his grandmother though he is away most of the week at college.

"Why, what a nice surprise. Come in, come in, we'll have some tea."

This is the same effusive friendliness the director used to suspect and now knows to be spurious. "This is not a social call." She hands the paper to the grandmother. "Have you seen this? Andy has been directly implicated in the writing of it."

After she reads it, "Oh, I know my grandson wouldn't do a thing like this. Now, won't you have some tea?"

"Nevertheless, Alice Wheeler has stated that Andy, along with others, dictated this to her. And she said that in the presence of witnesses, the Principal and Mrs. Baily, the advisor for the paper."

The grandmother begins to make anxious movements with her fingers revealing she has knowledge, or doubts, which she does not share.

"There's just some mistake. I know Andy wouldn't do something like this—the very idea is absurd!"

"When will he be home?"

"This afternoon about three."

"Ask him to come see me."

"Oh, I will—and I'll come too!" she says brightly.

"I prefer talking to him alone—but that's up to you."

The next morning, since Andy hadn't shown up, the director calls the grandmother who, confidence restored, assumes her usual unctious tone.

"Well, I asked Andy and he didn't know a thing about it—hadn't even seen the paper!"

"I asked that he come to see me."

"He would have but he didn't know where you live!"

"Even though he's been here before?"

"Now you listen. None of this happened. You're just paranoid and imagining..."

The director hangs up.

And a short time later Mr. Wheeler, whom she's learned since yesterday is a deacon in the Baptist church, arrives in his truck and honks the horn. When she refuses to go out to the road, he and his wife come to the porch where she meets them and invites them in.

"I won't go in your house!" says Mr. Wheeler.

"You lied to me!" says his wife belligerently.

Puzzled at this change of mood, the director says there must be some misunderstanding and suggests they go in, sit down and discuss it.

"My boy didn't do anything to you!" blurts the wife,

glancing at her husband for approval.

"And if you don't stop harrassing that poor old woman,.,"

"What old woman?"

"Andy's grandmother, that's who! She told us you've been harrassing her these past..."

"But I called her on the phone this morning because..."

"...few days and if you don't stop," he shakes his fist at her, "we'll report you to the Elderly Abuse people!" Whereupon they both stomp off, Mr. Wheeler turning back to issue another warning. "You'd just better be careful!"

She decides she will not confront the others involved. Immediate and present danger she thinks, and gets up to check that the doors are locked. But if and when danger, the vigilantes come, it will be night, not day. And what can she do to protect herself? She has installed locks on all the doors and as added insurance should the doors be forced, attached bells to each.

How exactly, did vigilantes attack? She tries, without success, to remember movies or books she has read. Calling the sheriff would be futile. Even if he came it would probably be too late. She thinks of calling the state police for she's heard they are generally more responsive, more competent and certainly less political. But though she's inquired she hasn't gotten a definitive answer as to whether they would come or merely refer the call to the sheriff.

Lastly, compelled again to look at this preogative, though she knows she will not use it, she could leave. First, the practicalities: where could she go? and where go with the cats? For they, too, are in danger. But the deciding factor, as always, is her rejection of either fight or flight . Fighting, becoming an aggressor, is not in her behaviour vocabulary so she would fail. Fleeing, whether by denial or literal flight, would turn her into a victim, something which, though victimized, she has refused becoming. Flight would also mean an acknowledgement of the depth of her fear. And she knows that, once she allows herself to recognize that, there is no returning, she will be lost forever.

She calls her lawyer who tells her she has done all the "right" things and thinks she need not fear a vigilante or any other action against her. She is not reassured by what she considers both his callousness and his ignorance.

• • • •

As stated, established attitudes which preclude learning or being modified by new information are properly called habits. And habit spawns oppression i.e., if we encounter ninety-nine white rabbits all of whom are ferocious, when we meet the hundreth rabbit we will oppress it with our belief that it, too, must be ferocious.

The oppressed's very survival depends upon their being able to forget (and we have already established that the obliteration of memory is tantamount to the formation of habit) their former self, to forget the experience of freedom, and what it was to be a respected and esteemed member of society. Hence we speak of the numbing or deadening effect of oppression for it does indeed murder the vital spirit of the person, leaving nothing but the habit of living.

The pain of oppression in people is mitigated, in small measure, where it is a shared experience. Oppression of an individual, in isolation, where there can be no commiserating, no exchange of storys of outrage, no affirmations of injustice, means that the screws are tightened considerably. Rage, the normal response, can find no safe target outwardly. But it can be turned inward. There never was an oppressed individual who did not, at dawn and dusk, contemplate suicide.

Fortunately or unfortunately, there are symbolic methods of suicide, perhaps the most common being murder of the spirit as mentioned before, whereby the person becomes a mere shell containing habits. There is also identification, often seen in hostages, where the oppressed merges with the oppressor, sharing attitude and convictions previously antithetical to them,even to the point of agreeing that they deserve to be victimized. Black slaves who gave up their endemic religion and took on that of their masters is a less inclusive version of this.

More chilling is the embracing of the oppressor where

he/she becomes, to all intents and purposes, a love object. For love and hate, with equally large components of obcession, are easily confused. And in a pathetic reach for health, the positive rather than the negative expression is chosen.

And finally, there is total obcession with the oppressor. Not the extreme preoccupation which occurs during the victimization, since this is necessary for survival, but persistence after the tyranny is terminated. For instance, the need for a new, felicitous ending sends some Jews back to Germany many years after the Holocaust in an attempt to release them from the past while, alas, they are clinging to it.

All of the above methods of coping with extreme circumstances carry danger, and no psychological treatment has been devised to guarantee remedy. We are well advised, then, to eliminate the circumstances, rather than attempt to treat the effects.

•   •   •   •

January, 1988
Sheila comes to visit and I teach her, somewhat impatiently, Für Elise on the piano. She has forgiven me for asking if she brought anyone into my house when she fed my cats during my absence and is, apparently, even more indignant in her defense when people in the community denigrate me. I try to relieve her of this burden of being my apologist by telling her the truth: it's of no concern and little interest what people here say about me. But a twelve-year-old's need for approval makes it impossible for her to imagine this immunity. On every appropriate occasion, I suggest she must go away to college when the time comes, the further the better, hoping to add to her discontent by telling her how much nicer are people in other places.

February, 1988
After two months without incident, hope began to take hold that my long ordeal might be over. But today G. comes

along while a friend is cutting up firewood for me from trees taken down by the power company last summer. I am working with him, gathering and stacking. G. stops, starts yelling, backs his truck up to get the wood I'd stacked while Jack, the friend, tries to point out the nearby survey marker to him and suggests that if G. needs wood he, Jack, would be happy to cut some for him on his own property. Thoroughly disgusted, I simply walk home to get away from it.

March 1, 1988
Having heard that the SW Chapter of ACLU has a new president, I apply to her by mail, reviewing my past experience with that chapter and telling of worsening situation since then.

March 26, 1988
G. sets several fires on my property. I go to sheriff's office and talk with Sgt. Thomas, whom I generally see now because if I insist on seeing the sheriff it usually means a wait of an hour, frequently two, standing in the vestibule because there are no chairs (this clear message of "don't bother us" is reinforced by the attitude of the personnel). Sgt. Thomas tells me that if G. sets any more fires to call him immediately and they'll pick him up.

April 1, 1988
No response from ACLU president but after many attempts, I'm able to reach her by phone. She, Peggy, thinks it "something they should get involved in" and will get in touch with me next week.

April 8, 1988
G. brushhoggs property. Bettina is here. I've asked her, too, to keep a log of the things she witnesses—though I've long lost hope that mine or hers will have a chance to prove of value. For me, though, it's become a habit to record incidents.

April 9, 1988

G. knocks down the temporary posts I'd set up in order to string a wire to define my property lines. Sheriffs office notified, deputy comes out to investigate, I point out where G. brushhogged and set fires.

April 12, 1988

Posts set up again, this time in concrete. G. comes with truck and knocks them over before they've had a chance to set thoroughly. Call sheriff's office, sheriff unavailable so I leave message.G.comes back and knocks over few remaining posts. No one from sheriffs office returns my call.

April 13, 1988

Go to sheriffs office to tell him of most recent events. I ask him why, since G. has repeatedly trespassed, damaged property, threatened and harrassed me for the past two years, why he, the sheriff has done nothing. He does not like this direct question. He stutters a bit then says the land boundaries are not clear. I ask why he has chosen not to accept the assessor's word, the abstract company's word, the results of the new survey. He says he was not aware that the new survey was finished. I ask if he does not remember my giving him a copy of the new survey last June, telling him of my concern because a fire had been started on my property (I couldn't accuse G. because I had not seen him set it) right after the survey was completed and that since I was going away for a week I was worried. And further, did he not remember that he had told me "something was going on in the village which needed watching anyway" so he would have a deputy make a run past my property occasionally. He says he did not remember this. I ask him why he has done nothing about the assault. He does not reply. Finally, pressed, he says that "now the property boundaries are clear" he will see the prosecutor this afternoon and that they will issue a summons to G. and "get this matter settled once and for all". I ask if he has any idea how many times in the past two years I have been told this very same thing. He does not reply. I ask if there is any reason I should believe him this time. He does not reply.

April 18, 1988
Again called Peggy, the ACLU president, who apologized for not getting back to me. She said she was embarrassed about how that chapter had treated me before, and explained that they were dependant upon volunteer lawyers, who were not always competent. She said that Ruark, the one who handled it before, had "serious personal problems" (hardly news) and she would not use him again. In light of this, and because she does not believe the other lawyer in the chapter is competent either, she has been trying to locate a local firm who will accept cases on a contingent fee basis since she has two other cases which require quick and competent handling. Because she thinks my case "political", she recommends the large, established firm of W.F. because they are immune to local politics and do take contingent fee cases. Says she has also been considering the Kansas/Western Missouri chapter to see if they can handle the case. My previous experience with them leads me to tell her quickly that I prefer the W.F. firm and I'll let her know if they accept the case.

Since harassment continues here unabated, and I have no faith the sheriff will finally act, she says she will call and tell him the ACLU is concerned about my receiving due process. She thinks this will make him act, and that if G. knows action against him is pending he will leave me alone until that time when lawyers can start procedures on my behalf. After hanging up the phone, I dance around the room, tears of relief burning my eyes. At last, at last, I think, something will be done, something *is* being done, I am no longer alone. Life seems, suddenly, worth living. Later, on a walk down Strawberry Road, I feel safer, almost confident.

• • • •

Lest this sound too negatively biased a report, further mention should be made of the positive aspects of habit.

When a disaster of major proportions occurs, such as an earthquake or tornado, the habit of consideration serves as an impediment to heedless, impulsive behaviour such as is found in mob reaction. We then speak of people acting "civilized", though we have no basis for assuming primitive man was inconsiderate—and actually many indications of thoughtful cooperation. Nor can we attribute such compassion only to homo sapiens since other animals display like concern for their own species: when a huntsman fires into a herd of elephants, for instance the others run *towards* the wounded one, not away.

Real compassion, that which is devoid of self-interest, is wedded to free will. Almost a century after William James struggled with the involuntary vs volition dichotomy, choosing finally to believe in free will, Phillip Slater described individual freedom's dark side. He wrote, " Like Kitty Genovese, you can be stabbed to death in front of hundreds and be confident that no one will stick their nose in your business."

We associate this "look-the-other-way" guarantee of personal freedom with urban living and assume it doesn't exist in rural areas. And probably in the time of James this was true. When the necessity of interdependence between rural folk was a recognized reality, looking the other way was not affordable. Instead, cooperation, such as sharing expensive farm equipment, was an habitual way of regarding relationship with ones neighbors. A habit of compassion, if you will.

•   •   •   •

April 20, 1988
Returning home with two ninety pound bags of concrete mix, I decide to remove the logs from my drive rather than transfer the concrete to the wheelbarrow and push it the 300 yards from the residents house. I park my car on the road while I'm removing the logs. But while struggling with the logs, G.'s wife comes along and without thinking, out of the habit of consideration, I go back to my car and move it so she can get past. Which she does without

even a side glance towards me.

April 21, 1988
I witness G. start a fire on my property. Reluctant to call local fire company since I've learned the chief was implicated in the article in the school paper, I call the Conservation Dept. instead. Try to put the fire out myself because they haven't shown up and the wind is blowing towards the residents house but I can't control it so do call local fire dept. and they put it out just about the time the Conservation truck arrives—they had gotten lost. Call Sgt. Thomas about the fire who says if I will come in Monday morning at 9 AM to make a complaint they will get a warrant. Checking my log I see he told me on March 26 that if G. started another fire to call and they would "pick him up". If he puts me off again on Monday, I'll remind him. It occurs to me too, that I should let them know about the log, that I'm recording everything-including my calls to them, whether, and how they respond.

April 22, 1988
Witness G. start another fire. Call Sgt. Thomas again. Remind him of what he said in March and ask to get protection over the weekend because I fear G. will do more damage. He says they can't do anything without a warrant.

April 25, 1988
Meet with Sgt. Thomas who questions me about fires. This usual question: "were there any witnesses?" to which I automatically respond: "Yes, me," and to which they look blank I can never get used to. It's as though I didn't exist. Somehow, if I say it, it isn't true or it's questionable; if someone else says it, it becomes "true". Yet other things I say are accepted as truth without question. And what do they think? That living in the country, you of course have a witness present at all times?
I write a formal complaint. He asks me to confine it to the last two incidents of fire only. And now he tells me that he had also asked G. to come in at the same time.

Obviously he didn't, and Sgt. T. says in an ironic tone "I wonder why". Does he think I like being tricked like this any better? And what's the point anyway?

I ask for a copy of the complaint but he says that as soon as the paper work is done he will give the complaint to the prosecutor who will then obtain a warrant from the court and G. will be arrested. I ask how long this will take. If the prosecutor is available, the warrant issued right away, action would be complete in two days, he says. If the prosecutor chooses to review the material, then it might be longer. I tell him I'm concerned for my safety when G. is again released. He promises to call me when G. is picked up and again when he released so I can take precautions. I point out that every time I've made a complaint, G has retaliated, "*This* time," he says. "Well stop him once and for all."

Why do I have such a strong feeling that something sinister, something "behind the scenes" which will be of no benefit to me, is going on?

April 28,1988
Sgt T. calls to say all papers are on prosecutor's desk and marked urgent. Yet my feeling of unease is stronger despite this apparent progress. And I don't think it has anything to do with how G. might react.

May 4, 1988
Today G. brushhoggs my property. It's now three weeks since I spoke with the sheriff and he promised to see the prosecutor that afternoon and get a summons issued for G.; it is now seven days since my complaint marked urgent was placed on the prosecutor's desk.

May 5, 1988
G. brushhogged again more extensively. Call sheriffs office, both he and Sgt. T. unavailable. Also called Peggy. She had called the sheriff two weeks ago (ah, maybe this is why Sgt. T. is so accommodating?) At first, the sheriff told her that I'd never made a complaint, then changed that to I'd never made

a *criminal* complaint (I used the forms given me) and that when I'd come in I was so incoherent that try as they might they could never tell what was going on. So they just figured it was two crazy people squabbling over land. She believes he is scared now, and covering up, but will probably act. She told him that ACLU's interest was not concerned with who was right or wrong but making sure I got due process. And she pointedly mentioned a *writ of mandemus* (court order for a public official to act), said she would call him again in two weeks to find out what action had been taken.

Aha, I think, this explains the flurry of activity here. And yet, and yet ... something smells wrong.

Peggy tells me to make a written statement of all criminal acts which have occurred in the past two months, have this notarized, and hand-carry copies to the sheriff and prosecutor. Since her two weeks warning is up today she will call the sheriff and also the prosecutor to threaten him too with the *writ of mandemus*.

She warns me that things may get "hot" in the next few days and tells me to make copies of *all* papers concerning the case and put them in a safe place *not my house*, she emphasizes. This sounds a bit over-dramatic to me. I'm thinking no more danger than usual, but I do what she says. I feel very invigorated, things are happening, my nightmare coming to an end.

And yet .... something ...

May 6. 1988
Hand-carry notarized copies of complaint to sheriff and prosecutor. Since the prosecutor is out of town I place it in the hands of his secretary. Also send a copy to Peggy. Peggy calls. She had tried to call the sheriff but was told he's out of town. I ask her what time she called. It turns out it was about the same time I was handing him the complaint.

She pauses, then says there is a complication. I hold my breath. She has heard that the prosecutor is on the Board of Regents of the college where she works for the president.

64

If she verifies this, she says, she will have to be very circumspect in her handling of this lest her job be compromised. I tell her that I've heard he is indeed on the board. In that case, she says, I can't do the *writ* but that any other lawyer can do it. I point out that I don't have a lawyer and that all I've approached here won't accept the case. She hesitates then says look, even *you* could do it, and quotes prior cases which involved conspiracy between public officials and defendant, tells me to check the statutes. I ask if you don't have to establish intent in a conspiracy. She says intent is implied by an act or failure to act. But then she says no, I shouldn't do it, I should get help with it.

Hesitating again, she says that though she is a lawyer she is not licensed to practice in Missouri—only in California so she cannot give me legal advice. I ask if the KC Chapter can't help with this. Her reply is vague, but then she says she will call them on Saturday and get their advice. She asks about the W.F. firm, I tell her I've written them, called, but keep getting put off because the case hasn't been assigned yet. She tells me not to call her at her office anymore, this places her in too much jeopardy. She gives me her home phone number. I assure her I'm concerned she not be compromised and will be discreet, but point out that I've already put her name on the complaint form as president of the ACLU, "by advice of". She is suspicious of the road which runs through my property and dead-ends at G.'s house. Tells me to check my abstract to find out whether a Right of Way was ever granted, then go to commissioner to find out if it actually is a county road as I've been told.

May 11, 1988
Peggy calls to say she has not contacted sheriff or prosecutor again because she is still concerned about how she can handle *writ* without getting herself into trouble. She tells me to go to the prosecutor, wear a dress, act dumb and helpless and ask if my land can't be posted by order of sheriff to keep G. off. Mention the *writ* casually, she says,

saying that ACLU wants to do it but I've told them to hold off because of "publicity, embarrassment, etc." At least from this, she says, we'll get some idea of his thinking, how adamant he is, and this will help in planning strategy. While we are talking about this I am laughing, but later find the whole thing, conspiracy within conspiracy, distasteful. Perhaps lawyers are used to this sort of thing. Nevertheless, I call to make an appointment. His secretary says the prosecutor has not yet read the complaint and will contact me for an appointment when he has.

May 12, 1988

A virtuoso guess—Peggy is right about the road Though it runs across my property, no ROW or compensation ever granted. In addition, there's no stop sign where the road meets the highway, mailboxes are at the highway rather than in front of the houses—all indications it's not a county road. Commissioner says it *is* a county road, that they grade it (but they grade it only 2-3 times a year, not regularly like other county roads). He seemed a bit nervous, overstating his case. And now I remember neighbors telling me that G. pays to have it graded so I ask county clerk who tells me that would be illegal. Check out statutes regarding the establishment of roads as county roads. It verifies that this is not one.

I'm uneasy. I remember now certain comments made by G. about the road which made no sense at the time because I thought it *was* a county road. Now I realize he knew it wasn't but wanted me to think it was. And the road, apparently, is of extreme importance to him. Why? Write a note to Peggy telling her what I've discovered.

The W.F. Firm notifies me my case has been assigned to Howath, with whom I've talked on the phone and to whom I've sent all material. They will give me their decision about acceptance of the case "within a week", he said. But now it's been 10 days so I call but he's always "unavailable" and doesn't return my calls. Tell his secretary my situation is *VERY* precarious, *PLEASE*.

Again call G.'s lawyer to ask that he prevail on G. to stop the harassment. lie says he will. I ask casually: "He's concerned about the road, isn't he?" He admits that's true. I say there seems to be some discrepancy. He says, "Oh, G. has a deed" and gives me the number. Go to courthouse and make a copy. It's a fraudulent deed since G. declares road passes only through his property. Essentially, he has deeded *my* property to the county. I have an uneasy sense that the information I'm getting puts me at high risk. And the irony doesn't escape me. Yes, an absurdity to "own" property ("my" property is still deeded to Colony) and now the property which I've taken pains to not "own" is being taken away from me. And by someone who is very skillful at it. Before Gus died and before all this controversy he told me that when he and G. used to have adjoining property they agreed on property line, purchased and installed together a fence on that line and during the night G. came and moved the fence a foot over on Gus' property. He and others in the community have told me that G. harassed "two old women" for 30 years before they finally made a quit claim, deeding over to him some 79 acres. I can't verify the first story but deeds suggest the second is true.

June 1, 1988
Still not heard from the prosecutor so call his office. Secretary says he has reviewed complaint and will not take action. I say I'd like to talk to him anyway. She leaves, comes back, and reports that if I want to see him, his consultation fee is $25. Illegal, of course, since he's a public official—Peggy goes through the roof when she hears this. Peggy tells me to go back to the commissioner and push again about the road. I have a feeling I'm weaving a web around my-self and it's getting tighter and tighter but I go back. At first he repeats it's a county road. As Peggy instructed, I say I'm still concerned for if it is a private road then I'm liable if an accident should happen on it. Ask if I can see a map showing county roads and he points out a

large map on the wall, I study it and point out that my road is not included. He gets very nervous, keeps referring me to the prosecutor, "he's my prosecutor and he's yours, just go see him". My hunch is that he's been given instructions-but only to a certain point. Then he says "now I know there's been trouble out there and I'm not taking sides—you just go talk to the prosecutor." That he "knows there's been trouble" verifies he's in prosecutors, G.'s, somebody's, confidence. I say casually that my lawyer has advised me to close the road before ... His reaction is immediate and explosive. He starts shouting that I can't close the road, I *can't!* Go ahead and *sue us*, he says, sue *us*! I say I'm not interested in suing anybody, just protecting myself from liability. He is very belligerent with his fear. I leave quickly.

What I've inherited is a history of citizens who never questioned authority, hence the authorities have not had occasion to become skilled at chicanery or, like the prosecutor, are so arrogant they won't waste the skill on me. And here this is a skill which is admired, not deplored. My audacity at forcing the issue only increases their rage. I realize now that everyone involved in this scenario knew about the road except me. The sheriff not only knew but knew I didn't know. I am having trouble breathing as I recognize that I have no control or knowledge of circumstances gathering around me.

June 28, 1988

The May 6th notarized complaint I placed in the hands of the prosecutor's secretary, the same complaint the prosecutor "reviewed" and "refuses to take action on" was returned to me today from the dead-letter office in Minnesota marked insufficient address. I had sealed and marked the envelope merely with prosecutor's name and county. Someone in his office placed it in a postal box. Someone in his office who doesn't want it known that he received the complaint. It would seem they are planning a strategy and need to cover up certain facts.

Report to Peggy my meeting with commissioner and prosecutor's tricks. She is shocked and angry, says we've got to get him for dereliction of duty. I cheer and ask ACLU? But she backs off saying well, if the W.F. Firm would get on the ball ... I tell her that Howath is a real dud. After two months, even though I've stressed the urgency, they haven't told me whether they'll accept the case, Howath doesn't return my calls and keeps making excuses when I catch him that he's "only a junior partner" and the "senior partners are to blame for the delay". She says she won't refer any more clients to them since, like me, they all need quick action.

Then she tells me to close the road. Just put up a fence or gate or something. Before questions arose about the road, I had another one made across my back meadow so I wouldn't have to unblock my drive each time. I tell her he'll just run through it with his tractor—nothing stops him.

Well, then, she says, BLOW IT UP!

And for one wild crazy moment a free space opens in front of me, a space I can step into with no fear, no fetters—a *wonderful* solution! After all, the road provides him access to bully me. The same road provides access to my night visitors. If the road were gone it would be like having a safety net around me. I could work again. Wouldn't have to jump up each time he passes or constantly listen for him. Not have to swallow my rage when he passes and leans out his window to grin and wave, his signal of triumph when he's gotten away with another piece of destruction. Why I could live my life ... I could live my life as though he didn't exist! What a glorious vision!

But then ... wait, aren't I required to give him notice before closing I ask, so he can arrange other access (his property borders another road so he does have a way out)? No, she replies, it's your property to do with as you want without having to notify anyone. I say I am very scared. If all, or even part, of what he's been doing for the past two years centers around the road then his fixation is psychotic—and his reaction to it's being blown up would also likely be psychotic. Anyway, I take a deep breath, more soberly, my guess is that it would not stop the harassment, just make it more inconvenient. She agrees. I am deflated. I tell her I am very discouraged. For a while it seemed possible, even plausible, there would be a resolution but everything has come to a screeching halt. She is sympathetic, but non-committal.

July 20, 1988

I go consult Davidson about closing the road. He strongly advises against it. He used to be prosecutor in another county and says that when anyone put up a barrier he simply ordered a grader to go out and knock it down; if they put it up again, he ordered the grader out again. "Even when the private citizen was acting within their legal rights?" I asked. He merely shrugged and grinned. Apparently all prosecutors must have their fun. He points out, as Peggy and I agreed, that the harassment would continue anyway.

July 21, 1988

Peggy calls to ask if I've made a decision about closing the road. Tell her what Davidson said, she expresses no opinion. G. continues brushhogging, etc., I tell her, and that though I sent the W.F. Firm the material they requested (a list of G.'s assets) more than a month ago and applied to them more than *three* months ago, no decision yet. She says to keep trying. I'm too depressed to talk further.

❂   ❂

Is it sufficient reason to stay because of the way light enters, graces this space? Still as awe-inspiring as my first season here. And while I can claim authorship for the walls, doors, windows, the very design, so pleasing to my eyes, I cannot really claim creation for the divine illumination.

While building this house I scribbled messages, perhaps a hundred, and tossed them into the cavity of the concrete block walls. The messages read: (1) Buddha, smile on this

70

house, (2) Buddha, smile on the people of this house. And, finally, after I caught on: (3) Buddha, smile ...

When I awaken before dawn these mornings I lie waiting for that first hint of light to visit. While waiting I re-live, through my body, the building process. Days, months, years of labor, despair alternating with intense satisfaction, my remembering body glows with sweat, my fingers ache with cold, remembering, and I smile ... smile ...

Then I hear G.'s truck start up. This reality, and the day, begins.

• • • •

Having suffered much from depression and noting that other of his siblings were also prone to psychological difficulties, William James, ever the responsible "oldest sibling", decided he should not marry lest he inflict pain on wife and perhaps children. But at the age of 36, after a few years of courtship, he mastered his equivocation and married Alice. He wrote later "I have found in marriage a calm and repose never known."

When James, at the age of 56, first began speaking about pragmatism as a philosophical principle, he was drawing upon the radical empiricism of John Stuart Mill, Locke and Bergson. James believed that the "truth" of an idea is not stagnant; truth *happens* to an idea, truth *becomes* true, is *made* true by events. Thus truth, like experience, perhaps like the cosmos itself, is always emerging, going through transformations. He distinguished between pragmatism and radical empiricism by pointing out that the latter holds that all knowledge is derived from experience and the testimony of the senses, while pragmatism is a method of thinking i.e. using ideas as instruments of thought.

That empirical experience of calm and repose he found in his marriage did not, alas, protect him from bouts of depression throughout his life. One might say that he never established the habit of being calm.

• • • •

71

G. brushhogging again. When I tell him to get off my property he ignores me as usual. Start throwing rocks at his tractor, one bounces off and hits him on the arm. He stops, gets off his tractor, starts toward me. I back off, not sure what to do. He yells he will report me for hitting him with a rock and I yell back, "Good! tell them what you were doing when it hit you!" He gets back on his tractor and continues the brushhogging.

· · · ·

Sometimes an organism under great stress will stubbornly continue habits though they no longer "make sense". The widow cooking for two, Lady Macbeth and her hand-washing, the lion pacing his cage over and over so the concrete floor becomes worn to a path. Such activity is not purposeful. We see this phenomenon in efforts not involving the physical body as well, such as in the habitual liar who lies when there is nothing to be gained by it. And it is our habit, when we see such behavior, to impose on it a meaning, a purpose, a motivation where none exists. An attempt, if you will, to tidy things up, make "sense" where there is none.

Our neighbor scrubs her sidewalk every morning and we assume she is over-fastidious or is expecting her mother-in-law; our landlord sprays monthly the whole apartment building with pesticide and we label this activity a cautious, preventative measure; a man beats his wife routinely, refuses her medical attention when she's ill and we interpret this to mean that she owns the family fortune and he is seeking her early demise. But the scrubber may have no purpose, the pesticide-spraying no meaning, the beating no motivation, and except for a slight reduction in tension released by the motor activity—just as might the administration of a drug temper the pain of addiction, these actions may be undertaken as ends, not means to an end.

· · · ·

When Howath called me a couple of weeks ago he told me that if I would ascertain G.'s assets for them, the W.F. Firm would consider taking the case on contingency. I quickly agreed and asked how I could do that.

"I haven't the slightest idea," he replied.

"But then how do *you* get such information?"

"Oh. we have special investigators for that."

"And how do *they* do it?"

He laughs. "I don't know and they wouldn't tell me if I asked."

A conundrum that I whittle away at for the next few days. Obviously it can be done because the investigators do it. And probably the way they do it is illegal or they wouldn't be so reluctant to talk about it.

Bit by bit, I build a stratagem.

Making up a story, I call a realtor, describe G.'s house (on occasion, before this began, I'd taken tomatoes, apples, etc. of which I had an abundance, to G.'s wife who had invited me in once briefly so I was acquainted with the interior of the house) the other buildings and property, and she gives me a range for the market value. Known in the community as a skinflint, I expect G.'s savings to be substantial, guess which bank he would use, call and identify myself as clerk at a farm implement business in the next county, explain that G. is there wanting to purchase an implement for $12,000. and ask if he has enough to cover this?

"In which of his accounts?"

"Uh, hold on, I'll ask him."

A moment while I think. "Uh, he's way out in the yard, I'll have to send someone out to ask. . ."

"Hold on."

It seemed a long wait.

"Yeah, he's fine."

So at least $12,000. in one. Why two? or even more? Is one a joint account? Howath had told me that joint accounts can't be touched. But from his reputation of considering all money his, not to be shared by his wives (this is his third—both previous ones having died, the community asserts, from lack of medical care) and since the teller didn't mention joint, it probably isn't.

Try as I might I can think of no way to find out his savings. But already we've got $99,000 for sure, counting property and the bank account. It takes me another few days to figure out how to get an estimate on crops, livestock and equipment. Then it comes. Of course: go to the source.

I write a script for myself, practice it, using a strong hillbilly accent, then nervously call another local, for practice, who has cheated me on several occasions. The ruse works even better than I'd expected so after more rehearsal I call G.

"Is this Mr. Lem Grass?"

"Gross," he corrects.

"Mr. Gross, my name is Mrs. Ashcroft and I'm with Gov'ner Stanford's Task Force to encourage Missourian's to purchase Missouri products-including farm products—I'm sure you've read or heard about that?"

"Well, uh, yes—I don't know a lot about it but..." The magic of the "Govner's"'name is already working. Never before have I heard this man express anything but absolute certainty. Nevertheless, my nervousness persists. I keep expecting him to say "all right, I know who this is."

"Well, we're right happy with our efforts so far and now we're doing this survey to confirm our success. Would you mind answering a few questions for us?"

"Why, sure, if I can..." What, *modesty* in this bully?

"Now let me just get my list. Now do you own your own home, Mr. Grass uh, Gross?

"Yep, sure do. My pappy had it. Now it's mine."

"And you have how many acres there, Mr. Gross?"

"342." Pride in his voice.

"And is the soil such that you can raise crops on some of that?" I relax and begin to have fun. One by one G. answers all questions on my list: what equipment, estimate of its worth, which crops and what payback he expects—all of this he answers with great eagerness.

When I ask if he has livestock, he replys, "Only my wife", and laughs heartily.

"Oh, you're such a card, Mr. Gross!" I respond, and see him repeating this whole conversation at the town diner tomorrow morning.

I feel quite sure that had I inquired, "Now Mr. Gross, if I were to sue you for what you're worth how much could I be expected to get?" he would surely have told me. Those investigators had nothing on *ME*.

August 7, 1988

Not quite willing to give up closure of the road and what that could mean to me, yet too afraid to carry through, I decide to test the wind. Put up a sign stating road will be closed but no date by order of owner. Make two signs since I expect G. to tear down the first one—hopefully I can get a picture of him doing it as he has all the no trespassing signs. Then I'll put up the other sign, let him tear it down. This will prepare him somewhat, and give me a gauge of how crazy this makes him.

August 19, 1988

G. sets fire to brush near my mailbox. My tenant (I've rented the residents house for the summer) puts it out, then tells me.

August 23, 1988

G. brushhoggs again today.

August 26, 1988

Go in sherriff's office to file a complaint about fire and brushhogging. Dispatch deputy tells me they "don't want any more complaints from you. We're not going to do anything anyway." At first she refuses to give me a complaint form but when I tell her I'll use my own paper, she hands it over. When I finish and hand it back, she simply rolls her eyes.

Drive home over my old road since the new one is too muddy. My car is overheating, (it's 98 degrees today) about to boil over, so I park it on the road in front of my house in the shade to let it cool off.

○   ○

Months have passed since the article appeared in the school newspaper (her retraction was never printed and when she went back to confront the Principal he told her he thought it wiser and safer for her to drop the matter). After some thought, she did. For the discovery, one by one, of those in the village who were directly or indirectly involved led her to recognize and set aside her naivete, then reassess the terrain.

In the foreground are those who openly act against her. The middle ground consists of those who abet those actions or, it can be guessed, encourage them behind the scenes. Finally, in the background, are those whose encouragement is passive, i.e., they are aware, don't necessarily condone, and excuse themselves by carefully looking the other way. She believes, on evidence, that every member of the community fits into one of these categories.

Since it is impossible, because of their facile hypocrisy, to tell in which category fits this person who is greeting her so warmly, she cuts off all contact with the villagers to protect herself from the pain of continuous betrayal. And, as always, continues to work towards an understanding of why all this is happening.

And finds: given the probable personal history of G. and most of the others here, their victimization in all forms of abuse, how could they be other than what they are? For in the midst of their pain resulting from the physical, sexual and psychological abuse, they are handed a religion which promises to deliver them from their agony. A formula—for that is what fundamentalism—which guarantees that God is love (yet cruel), insists that people are intrinsically sinners (hence deserve any punishment they get) and that they will be liberated from their tortured and torturing hatred if they will only embrace these contradictions with heart and soul. So, trusting and desperate they fall to their knees in supplication, only to discover they have been handed the coup de grace—a religion which does not work. This final insult, a god who is fickle and silly, in whom they cannot believe yet must profess to believe, a god whom they loathe in secret but to whom they are married forever, a habit like a second skin—into this seething morass steps a person not only free of all these constrictions but who wears her freedom, casually, like a cloak of no consequence.

No wonder, then, that G. will not be satisfied until she "gets down on her knees," grovels in the mire with the rest of them. For what is on trial here is not the director, not the people of the community, not religion, but freedom itself.

In an effort to trigger genuine outrage in the homesteaders she had told them that freedom doesn't come in bits and pieces, scattered among the few. If I ain't got it, you ain't either, she told them. But as George Bernard Shaw insists, there is only one thing people love more than freedom and that is slavery. In fact, her experiences have confirmed that as soon as people get a glimpse of freedom they become terrified, seeing it as a freefall, no safety nets. To save themselves they grab anything, a dust mote, a crumbling ideology, a religion replete with nonsense. A habit. Anything which creates the illusion of separateness, such illusion necessary for attachment to occur. So, clinging to this thread of delusion, convinced it is firmly attached to a wall of security, they dangle happily while keeping their eyes averted from the abyss below.

But to follow the "if I ain't got it you ain't either" argument, should not her first move be to assure G. and the others *their* freedom? For if the word is to have any meaning G. must be free to be what, to her, is a son-of-a-bitch. And if we circumscribe a boundary beyond which the son-of-a-bitching must not extend, then are we not abridging freedom? Or, at best, setting limits on that which by being limited disappears? The old freedom, your fist-my-nose equation is too simplistic to serve. On the other hand, she is wary of the "liberal" stance whereby understanding the adversary's point of view leads to empathy, with the result that you become paralyzed to act, whilst granting the other free rein. No, that way promises no resolution merely a continuation of victimization

Well, then: a koan. Not to be acted upon until solved. And not to be "solved" by rational means but by a transcendent leap. Not to claw ones way up and over the wall, nor laboriously tunnel through it, but to simply walk through the gate.

Mostly though, she has lost interest in why; she wants, needs, an ending. Or a means to an end. Turn the other cheek, non-violent resistance, application to those agencies designed to handle such transgressions—none of these have worked.

For instance the non-violent resistance. Even Ghandi said that it had worked for India only because, at heart, the British were a decent people. She did not have that luxuriant gift. In her eight years here she had not seen a single act of kindness among the villagers.

And even if they kill her? And she doesn't think this is what they want, for what fun in prodding a dead body? No, they want her to become what they call her: a witch, manifesting all, and only, evil. Breathing fire from her mouth. Haunting the director's vision of G. is an incident which occurred some years ago, long before the present trouble. Though she has tried to banish it, it sticks, perpetually peripheral. Like the first faint appearance of the evening star which one detects not by looking directly at it but to one side.

She had been raking leaves in her yard, pausing occasionally to gaze out over the panorama of hills in front of her where the grasses and foliage were beginning their first subtle transformation into autumn brilliance. G. came by on his tractor—not then a cause for concern, and they waved at each other. The day before, trucks had come for the fattened cattle, leaving the pasture empty except for the lone bull now standing in a grove of trees near the pond. Was he grieving? puzzled? worried? nothing? Whichever, he obviously was in the wrong place for G. stopped his tractor, leaving the motor running (very unusual and what attracted her attention), mounted the fence, approached the bull and very gently started coaxing it down the hill towards the barnyard. What arrested her was the gentleness. She had had enough experience of G. by then to find any tenderness, particularly towards animals, surprising. And, if she were to find credence in the stories she'd heard, that G. casually killed the pets of people he was angry with, then his present behavior was even more puzzling.

All went well for a while, the bull docilely moving in front of G. down the hill. Then she was momentarily distracted and apparently missed an episode for when she next sees G. he is in his truck, in a distant part of the field closely tracking the bull, with the tractor still running in the road. Something alarms her—perhaps the still-running tractor? the closeness of the tracking? and she stands rigid, watching. As the scene unfolds on the vast arena before her it takes on an epic quality, the ritualistic reenactment of mans ancient and arrogant cruelty. Almost against her will she stands watching, realizing at the same time it is something she does not wish to witness.

The bull is not walking fast enough for G. so he prods it with the truck, the bull stumbles, G. pushes on. The bull moves towards a grove of trees for protection, G.'s truck heads it off, pushing harder and faster against the bull's rump. Now he has the animal running at a trot, though it is not clear whether the momentum is supplied by the bull or the truck. The bull stumbles, then stumbles again, and goes down. G. nudges it to its feet and the whole pattern is repeated again and again. Over the field they go, the direction seeming no longer to matter. If G.'s original intent was to get the bull in the barnyard, that intent is now consumed by his joy in the torture itself.

Several times the animal eludes him and reaches the relative safety of a group of trees, its sides visibly heaving now. But G. jumps out of his truck, leaving the door swinging, while he herds the bull away from his haven back into his line of attack. The bull is moving slower now and stumbling more frequently, the truck pushing its body several feet before it can regain its footing. The more drunkenly the bull moves the more, it seems, does G.'s enthusiasm increase.

The director moves herself away, walks down a path to examine a flower, gently touches her cat who lies sleeping in the tall grass, then returns to her vigil.

But the actors have disappeared, though the tractor remains running in the road. Then, from an area out of her sight down near his barn she hears G. shout, a shot, then another shot. Later, G. comes, gets on his tractor and continues down the road as though nothing of consequence has occurred.

With this scene playing peripherally, when she looks at G.she can no longer see him in his physical manifestation. Instead she perceives an assemblage of destruction: for face there is a young tree full of blushing cherries, a nubile apple tree modestly presenting its first-ever fruit, a pear tree plump with promise. His body is made up of amputated tree limbs, charred blooms of blackberries, fire withered wild flowers and wild strawberries, pesticide contorted foliage of various plants, hacked-off trunks and carcasses of trees. And there at the side, the bull, ever stumbling, rising to its feet and stumbling again.

August 30, 1988

Dear Peggy,

This is what happened. Two weeks ago I put up a sign on my road where it intersects the highway: THIS ROAD WILL BE CLOSED BY ORDER OF OWNER. Expected G. to tear it down but he didn't. In fact, it's still up. He had been busy that week, setting a fire and brushhogging. Friday when I went in to the sheriff to complain about that, they told me they wouldn't take any more complaints, they weren't going to do anything anyway. When I came home I took the gravel road (my new road was too muddy from recent rains). Almost in front of my house my car was overheating so I stopped before it boiled over, pulled to the side and raised the hood. I went in, intending to let it cool down before pulling it into my drive. A while later a truck went by and I looked out to make sure it could get by my car which it did without even slowing down. A red truck, so I assumed it was G.'s only realizing afterwards that it must have been Ronnie's, the guy who rents pasture from him. Not long after, G. comes up from his house followed by Ronnie in his truck. G. stops in front of my house, honks his horn for a while, which I ignore—then comes across the yard to my house, yelling: Bennett, Bennett! I'm sure this swagger was for the benefit of Ronnie, a young buck, a "see, I can still get it up, make the women cower" kind of thing. Of course this is unusual for him to get out of his truck or off his tractor because of the associated power. Really, this should have tipped me off to the danger but when he bangs on the door I open it. Get your car out of the road or I'll shove it! he yells, loud enough to make sure Ronnie can hear him. I tell him it's overheated, I'll move it later and he should go around as he did before. He yells that he won't, he's going to shove it. And I say well, in that case, I'll take your picture, I'm sure the insurance company will be interested if there's damage. And I grab my camera which I keep by the door. As you know, that's my "weapon." I stupidly follow him out to the road and lean against my car, camera ready. But he surprises me. Before I know what's happening, he throws

81

me down on the road and the camera goes flying. Then he grabs rocks and starts to beat me with both hands.

I remember only pieces of what followed and am not sure about the sequence. It seemed to go on forever. I know he threw me down at least three times, probably more. Most of what I was doing was holding his arms up so he couldn't hit me with the rocks—but then he would kick me. Despite his 72 years, this guy is strong and wiry—but then he's been a farmer all his life. Once when he drops a rock, and bends down to get another, I push him back against the hood of his truck, holding up his arms with the rocks in them and I see he's panting—so I release his arms. He just starts hitting me again.

All through this Ronnie stands there in the road, watching, and once I yell at him "are you just going to stand there and watch?" I couldn't understand why he didn't stop G. His girlfriend is sitting in the truck watching too. Anyway, the last time G. throws me down and I am getting up very slowly now and can't see well, blood running down into my eyes, I've just gotten on my feet and Ronnie steps in, places his foot in the middle of my back and sends me flying. This time I stayed down. I think I could have gotten up but thought I'd better not, that they would kill me then. I think they shoved my car then. I wasn't exactly unconscious, just sorta out of it and trying to figure where I was in relation to their trucks because I thought they might run over me.

They got in their trucks and left, left me lying in the road. Where I stayed for I don't know how long. I became aware of the hot sun on my face and felt the sticky blood. Got up and went into the house and just walked around for some time, wiping the blood off. My legs, everything, seemed to be working OK—everything except my mind. Finally tried to call Bettina but she wasn't home. Then tried to call Charles, one of the homesteaders. He wasn't home either.

I just sat for a while. Everything seemed very slow. Then I called you. Since everything seemed to work OK I didn't call an ambulance as you suggested but did drive myself to the ER. Incredibly, they don't keep a doctor on duty or even on call so it was two hours before one came to examine me. In the meantime they took X-rays then had to repeat them because my blouse had metal buttons. I broke down and cried at that point—the technicians incompetence the final straw.

They kept trying to get me to lie down but my body simply would not bend, the only clue I had that I was maybe in shock. When the Doctor finally came, he made a very cursory exam, not even looking at the head wounds, just telling the nurse to clean all the abrasions on my arms, legs, face, neck, chest. I did ask about the pain in my chest, he looked at the X-rays, then said I might have hairline cracks in the ribs which wouldn't show on the films. After he left, it was the nurse who dressed my wounds and advised if I became nauseous or dizzy this might indicate a concussion and I should seek medical attention.

So I got off fairly easy I think. Learned some things: I'm his match in terms of physical strength and probably have more endurance. I am not his match however, in being capable of inflicting harm on another person. I could defend myself, but only to the point of inflicting harm. And while I'm glad to learn that I *can* defend myself, this having never been tested and something I think a lot of women worry about, the fact that I cannot be aggressive even under such circumstances means I'm even more vulnerable than I thought.

When the hospital released me, there was a deputy waiting to take a statement. We went out to their car for privacy, one deputy sitting with me in front, another in the back seat. I was very uneasy—nothing coming out of that sheriff's office has been good news for me, I'd just been at the mercy of two men and here I was. All I wanted was to go home, even if that wasn't safe. I was so tired. I described verbally what had happened then they asked me to go to the sheriff's office to make a written statement. I said no, I would come in on Monday and do it, but they persisted so I did, thinking when the hell has writing a complaint accomplished anything. And hadn't they just told me a few hours before that they wouldn't take any more complaints?

Didn't bother to ask for a copy—it's all futile anyway.

After I got home I called Bettina and told her what happened. Later she called the sheriff's office to find out what they were going to do, and the deputy said that G. had reported that I'd blocked the road with my car and when they'd tried to get by I'd attacked both of them with rocks. When she scoffed at this, he said, well, were you there?

As for the W.F. Firm, I've decided I won't go with them. What they offer is not much: Howath, who is incompetent and stupid (you've agreed with that) and though they have the data on G.'s assets (*my* work) they now say if I foot the bill for their preliminary investigation *then* they'll make a decision. So after dangling me for three months, if I'll write them a blank check, they'll consider representing me. I'll ask Davidson if he'll reconsider—though I don't have a lot of confidence in him. But I'm too tired to start at the beginning with another lawyer now.

Thank you for being available for me on Friday. I watch friends here and see their terrible frustration at having to stand by helplessly.

❂   ❂

I crouch down behind the bushes. It's not so much that I'm afraid they will hurt me if they find me as it is to avoid their SEEING me. Their Evil eye. I think of slaves—is this the reason for their lowered eyes? Not to show deference but to protect themselves from the evil?

❂   ❂

August 29, 1988

This morning, two commissioners, one of them the man I've already spoken with about the road, come to my door. They are both burly, and look like thugs. They tell me not to "obstruct the road again." I point out that (1) I was not obstructing the road since a truck went by it and (2) it's my road. "I take no sides," says the one, lifing his hands with a menacing grin and now I see that G. has come with them, is waiting in his truck on the road, "but—and this is a message from the sheriff: if you block the road again we'll come out and (he pauses pointedly) tow your car!" They get in their car and follow G. to his house where they remain for a half-hour. Later G. passes and in his familiar triumphant way leans out of his truck grinning and waving.

○   ○

My walk late at night is like a tattered piece of the fabric of freedom that I must hold on to. Stars and sky still exist; I need to know that. I venture to a place from where, hidden behind a tree, I can see the Baptist Church—and watch as the moon moves from cloud to cloud, the church pass from darkness to illumination to darkness again. In this chiaroscuro I see clearly that had it not already been invented, a god would be needed as a repository for peoples responsibility, that as soon as the concept of God enters, then is evil conceived. And where people insist on a god, there evil exists.

○   ○

August 29, 1988
I go to Davidson to ask he re-consider taking my case. He replies that, on the basis of the latest outrage (the beating) he will—on a contingent fee. I ask even though I have questions about his competency and am uneasy because of his obvious vicarious enjoyment when I, as he says, "stand up and talk back to the sheriff and prosecutor." As though to reciprocate for my implied confidence, he tells me that the prosecutor makes his living, apparently a very good living, by visiting accident victims in the hospital, setting them up, then having his partner handle the trial. A good plan because the prosecutor is very persuasive but inept in court. Davidson finds this personally distasteful but points out that it is not illegal. I ask him, since he considers the prosecutor a personal friend, if this will

85

compromise my case. He hesitates, then says he will have a lawyer friend from Kansas City handle it, they frequently make such exchanges.

"You know, J. (prosecutor) is a very charming guy", he says. I look in disbelief at his insensitivity. "No, really, if you met him socially you'd see that."
He promises to let me know in a few days whether he'll take the case.

August 30, 1988

G. comes on his tractor, four days after the beating, boldly moving up my driveway and brushhoggs all my property. I learn he has already mowed up by residents house with the tenants watching. He finishes, goes home briefly, comes back to clear a lane along the perimeter of my land back into the woods on which is neither his nor my property. A fire break? so he can set fire in my woods where the fire trucks can't go and where it will go undetected but contained by the break so it doesn't reach his property? While he brushhoggs I crouch behind bushes near my garage. I have my camera back and try to find gaps in the foliage big enough so the pictures will contain both him and his tractor. Around and around and back and forth he goes, again and again, mowing the same area over and over. Sometimes he stands as he moves, his hands resting lightly on the steering-wheel. Is he then an explorer, seeking new territory? A soldier, checking for landmines? or is his mind a jumble of twisted wires, habits globbed onto other habits, convoluted, short-circuited?
When the pictures are developed, only two reveal a figure in faded blue overalls and shirt standing upright on a battered red tractor, surrounded by a bower of blurred green foliage.

August 30, 1988

Tonight, about 11:30, after I'm in bed but not asleep, I hear footsteps crunching the gravel outside the garage then a cautious jiggling of the garage door as though to check if it's locked. Without turning on the light I immediately call the highway patrol. About twenty minutes later, sheriff's deputies show up. Though in an official car neither wear uniforms. They look like tweedle-dee and tweedle-dum, both balloon-shaped, their clothes looking as though slept in several days, the shirts too small to button over their enormous stomachs, the top buttons of their pants, by necessity, unbuttoned. I think, "Ah, L's Finest!" and for a moment am threatened with hysterical laughter, urged on by their utter earnestness. They listen while I describe what I heard then leave to search the area. Minutes later, a commotion on the porch makes me look out to see that a porch step has given way under one of them but he merely shakes his foot as though it were asleep and goes on to search. I think he's probably unperturbed because this happens often, and now the laughter does come and I'm glad they can't hear me. I'm controlled by the time they come back, reporting they found nothing. Then the state police show up—they had transferred the call since the deputies were closer—so now I know how that works.

<u>August 31, 1988</u>
This afternoon the county grades my road. Obviously they've made a special trip to do this and it's clearly meant as a warning. They also extend the width of the road, encroaching even more on my property. G. comes by afterwards, leaning out and grinning. Now, in his transcendence, he does this every time he passes, as does Ronnie, who also sticks his fist out the window and shakes it in triumph.

•   •   •   •

Though we spoke of habit being purged of memory, a seeming contradiction is the phenomenon of physiological or muscle "memory" whereby muscles react involuntarily in a known and predictable pattern. Dancers use this when their mind has "forgotten" the choreography but their body hasn't; athletes and pianists utilize it, often performing movements of great complexity requiring fine coordination, all apparently with the mind "absent." In response to stressful stimuli, the stomach muscles may tense, creating a chain reaction of reduction of blood supply to the digestive system, restricted peristalsis, with resultant distress. This distress makes itself known by discomfort or pain, the alarm system designed to alert the body to seek remedy before permanent harm is inflicted.

However, when the stressing agent is ever-present, the physiological responses constant, then the body/mind becomes habituated to the symptoms, the red light fails to come on, the damage continues in secret.

• • • •

September 1, 1988
Bettina calls. A couple of days after the beating she again called the sheriff's office demanding protection for me. Their response was "how do you know there *was* a beating?" She said a deputy took my statement at the hospital. "We don't know anything about it," they responded. Asked if they had questioned G., they said no, no reason to. Asked if I could get protection, they said sure, have her come in and sign a complaint. Disgusted, she got up enough nerve to call the Lt. Governor's (state ombudsman) office to appeal.

September 2, 1988
Sheila comes, very upset, having just heard about the beating. She and her grandmother were in the town diner while G. was there bragging that he had beat me up and would do it again if necessary. Other people found this very amusing so, encouraged, he continued that yeah, I'd put my car crosswise in the road to block them, came out and was beating them with rocks. First, he said, I turned her over my knees and gave her a good spanking (that got a big laugh) then he and Ronnie had to beat me up. Sheila and her grandmother got very angry and told everyone that I'm the "nicest person in town and if they'd just get to know me and stop telling stories about me they'd find this out."

September 3, 1988
People from Elderly Abuse Program come to see me, sent by the Lt. Governor's office. I had talked several times to the

Lt. Governor's assistant who had repeatedly tried to reach the sheriff but he was always "out of town" and doesn't return her calls. He must be very confident, perhaps riding on the prosecutor who is the Governor's regional campaign manager and "fair-haired boy." This interview with the Elderly Abuse people is mere token since the Lt. Governor is aware, as are they, that I'm too young to fit into the guidelines. However they do take information, say they will make a report for the Lt. Governor and the sheriff, then they offer some suggestions as to how to handle my fear that G. will repeat the beating.

September 4, 1988

Sheila comes again with her friend to see how I am. While I'm making them herbal tea which they've never had before I overhear Marlene, the friend, telling Sheila to never get into Bard's truck (a man in his 50's, a lay Baptist minister) because he would molest her. They mention two other men of similiar age whom it's better to stay away from, and I am astonished at the casual tone of these warnings. Apparently the common euphemism the men use is "if you're old enough to bleed then you're old enough to spank." Now I understand G.'s reference to "spanking" me, confirming there were sexual overtones to the beating. But Baptists are so screwed up sexually that *everything* has sexual overtones for them.

While we're drinking the tea, Sheila tearfully admits that she doesn't know how to handle what happens during coffee hour following the Baptist service. G. (others too, but G. is the most persistent) comes over to her and hugs her—acceptable behaviour in this context, though further conversation reveals that such hugging takes place almost exclusively between males in the 50-70 age range and nubile females—and while doing so he feels her breasts and buttocks. She says she's so embarrassed because people are standing around watching and she doesn't want to be rude by moving away from him.

I point out that he is, of course, being very rude to her and that it's perfectly acceptable for her to resist. She looks doubtful. I say if she can't manage that then she can always arrange for someone to be between them, treat it like a game and, in addition, she might "accidently" tromp on his foot. I've been aware that such behaviour, including incest, is common here and, while it's not condoned, it is treated more like an impropriety than as something reprehensible.

✪   ✪

During these past few days many small things, the short sweet song of a bird, a cat leisurly moving across the road, an apricot tinted cloud all carry that sharp distinctness of great significance. Music, too, has a strange clarity, reaching me unedited, unmodified, and unanalyzed. Despite the clarity these experiences seem to occur at a great distance. A search for transcendence? The law says we have a right to kill in self-defence.
"Who" is this law?
Profoundly disturbing: when I felt my life to be in serious danger, I could not kill to save it. Is that not indefensibly irresponsible?

✪   ✪

September 10, 1988
Lt. Governor's assistant calls to say she's finally talked with the sheriff. She is vague about his response but he claims there is no reason to prosecute. Since she is reluctant to expand on this I can only imagine the lies he told. She asks if I'd be willing to meet with G. and a mediation team from the University of Missouri (Columbia) Law School. I suspect they know how inappropriate this is—G. is hardly a likely candidate for mediation—but need to make some gesture. I reluctantly agree hoping that when this gesture fails they may offer something more substantial. Davidson still hasn't decided if he'll take the case. He keeps saying, "probably" and will tell me in a few days—then doesn't. I've run out of appeal sources. Tried Legal Aid again,

90

also State Human Rights—but they deal only with housing, employment. Wrote Gloria Steinem, with no response, Scott Simon of Weekend Edition, no response. Tried School of Journalism at University of Missouri, suggesting my story as a thesis for a grad student in investigative reporting—no response. Again wrote small and large newspapers—not printed. Even write Southern Baptist Convention: can they possibly intervene?"—nothing. I've had no further contact with Peggy at ACLU. It's clear she will not jeopardize her job with any meaningful action, and it's long past the point when emotional support is sufficient.

October 7, 1988
A member of the Friends Meeting in Rolla (50 miles from me) refers me to a lawyer there whom I see. He refuses the case on a contingency basis because the distance would make it too expensive, and for fee, because he does not believe it would resolve the issue. That's my gut feeling as well, but I'm interested in why this lawyer, who's much more thoughtful than others I've seen, thinks it useless to sue. He stares out the window some time before answering, then in a sad voice says that he originally became a lawyer because he thought it had something to do with justice. He gives a rueful laugh. I ask for suggestions. He is very quiet for a while.
"You could kill him," he murmurs. "Mind you, I don't advocate it, but..." he shrugs his shoulders.
I sigh. "Alas, it's not an option available to me."
He nods. Then suggests I do a series of small-claims suits against G. This will keep him off-balance and busy and, monetarily, I can recoup at least some of my loss. I point out this seems to invite retaliation and I'll have no protection. He has no answer.

October 25, 1988
I leave for a stay at a Zen Monastery in New York State. No magic occurs. I remember longingly the interim I spent here

a couple of years before as Tenzo (monastery cook). I would leave dawn zazen after the first sitting, going down into the big kitchen as the sun rose over Mt. Tremper, the quiet like a healing balm, preparing breakfast, listening for the closing chant above in the zendo, before moving the food into the dining room.

This time the quiet doesn't reach me.

I am careful that my sudden bouts of weeping don't occur when anyone is present. Though I'm not officially a student, I've had past interviews with the teacher and decide that I want to see him. But when I join the interview line, one of the senior monks bustles over to tell me I'm not elgible. I am shattered. Though I feel physically safe here, I now feel vilified and excluded. In the next few days I have several anxiety attacks, hyperventilating, with just enough warning to leave quickly if I'm with people. A couple of times though I'm caught on the stairs by a passing monk as I am hyperventilating. She asks if I'm OK, I nod, she passes on.

When I finally decide to seek an audience with the teacher through the head monk, whom I know from times past, she is obviously not anxious to see me. Several days pass after my petition before she has a "few moments" free. I am hurt by this insensitivity. Surely my pain is obvious and she knows me well enough to know I don't seek help for trivial matters. But all I get from her is what, because it's happened often before, I've come to refer to as the "tsk, tsk" response. It is not only useless, it is insulting. All it achieves is that the petitioned one can feel "responsive" and think she has dispensed the proper sympathy. All the while knowing sympathy is not what is sought.

She says she will speak with the Abbot, she believes he has some influence with the ACLU. Several days pass while she ignores my beseeching looks, and my day for leaving is close before she lets me know that, instead of arranging for me to see him, she has told him of my troubles and he has said that I should, simply, leave my place. Afterwards I wonder if she did indeed see him, or how my case was presented. It is hard to imagine he would be so cavalier, it is so at odds with what I know of him. And I do know him.

The night before I leave the monastery I have my first nightmare, one which will repeat many times but not until some seven months in the future. In the dream I am in imminent danger, try to call for help, experience some relief when I can make a strangled scream which awakens me partially. Then I awaken fully to total despair when I realize that even if I'm capable of calling for help, there is none. When I return I discover Sheila fed my cats only once during my absence. Bettina, checking, discovered this and took over the feeding. When I next see Sheila, she at first lies, then says that when she was here she "heard something or someone", got scared, and never returned. Now I realize that my need for her to keep integrity intact has made me deny what I've really known for a while—that she has already lost it. I now remember her telling her friend, within my hearing, what some boy had said about the low-ered level in the living room that it should be a "wading pool." Since he had never been to my house, unless at her invitation, she has been lying to me all along. I grieve for her then give her up. Now I am alone among enemies.

December 14, 1988

Today is mediation day. I have decided not to have a lawyer represent me; G. has insisted his be present. When I arrive I see the room is very small and will require me to sit close to G. I begin to hyperventilate and ask the two mediators if we can meet in a larger room. We move there before G. arrives.

I'm asked to begin and I recite the incidents of the past 2 ½ + years and that the outcome I wish from this meeting today is (1) G. stays off my property and (2) stops his harrassment.

G., no doubt at the insistence of his lawyer sitting next to him, admits for the first time the trepass and damage but claims, contradictorily, that the property is his. As usual, his "truth" shifts back and forth sometimes in the same sentence, claiming at one moment that everything I've said is a lie, then in the next admitting he did these things. Not

93

the beating though. He clings to his story that I beat up both men. When asked by one mediator if he had sustained any injuries, he replied yes, his knee had been skinned, skinned bad, he added.

All shortly agree that nothing is to be gained here, the mediators ask me to stay and after G. leaves, tell me to start a suit against G. When I explain my lack of funds and that every lawyer I've seen refuses the case on contingent fee basis or because they fear reprisal by the prosecutor, they tell me I should get a *pro bono* lawyer. When I ask if they know of any in the state of Missouri, they are silent. Then they tell me I should get a restraining order. But when I ask who would enforce it, again they have no answer.

In the next three weeks I see eight lawyers, all outside the county, most are 50 to 60 miles away. All but two refuse because, they say, they do business with the prosecutor. Dereliction of duty on the part of the prosecutor and sheriff (though none seem to fear the latter) will become evident no matter how the suit is handled, they claim, and the prosecutor is known widely for taking revenge. The other two refuse because the distance to the local court is too great to repay the time invested and will not take the case on contingency. One declared she would accept it but only if it included all three (prosecutor, sheriff and G.) and only in federal court with a cost of approximately $10,000. Davidson, after keeping me hanging for over a month, told me he wouldn't take the case. Too tricky, he said.

❂   ❂

The sheriff, after having been in office for 12 years, lost the election in November. Before doing limited campaigning for the newly elected sheriff, I apprized him of my situation. He seemed shocked, tells me he would have handled it differently. I believe him to be basically honest if not tempted too far. Which is probably as much as can be expected here. He is not very smart. But if one has to choose, better the first than the last?

94

Sometime between December 15 and January 10, papers concerning my case disappeared from my house. Luckily I still have copies of everything in another place (I had heeded Peggy's advice). As the sheriff leaves office in January it is discovered that he has removed (and presumably destroyed) a number of files, mine among them. When he's questioned about this he maintains he removed only files which identified informants. To protect them, he claims. No charges are brought against him. I give copies of my case to the new sheriff.

○   ○

January 19, 1989
Night visitors have been hitting hard this month. When they just pull into the driveway, don't turn off their motor, yell (come out witch!) then drive off, it's not too bad. But when they turn off their motor, and I hear a car door slam, I get very frightened.
I put a no trespassing sign in a bucket of rocks in my driveway but G. comes and knocks the bucket over with his truck. I put it back and the next time he destroys both bucket and sign. I try these incidents out on the new sheriff, then on the newly elected assistant prosecutor, explaining that though it appears trivial, it is merely the last of many, many, such events. Kingroe, the assistant prosecutor, indicates knowledge of the case, saying he feels conflicted: on the one hand he's a lawyer, yet the prosecutor is his boss ...
He does say that if they arrest G. for this latest, it can only be for a misdemeanor, he will be released in hours.

January 26, 1989
Write the newly elected Lt. Governor. Don't really expect help anymore—to get any response at all is acceptable. Making the request has become a habit. His response indicates he misunderstood this to be asking for a referral to a lawyer which, of course, he is prohibited from doing. I write again, clarifying. He responds the same way proving

his "misinterpretation" is deliberate.

Have decided to take the advice of the one lawyer (the sad one) and file several suits in small-claims court. Will do one, leave for a while to relieve stress, return and do another, etc. Kingroe offers assistance in writing these claims. Tell him I've put former resident's house up for sale to finance my relocation. It is clear to me, though I'm still not facing it squarely, that leaving for good is necessary—eventually.

February 23, 1989
File first claim and ask to be notified when summons is served so I can take precautions.

• • • •

In describing Post-traumatic-stress-disorder we pointed out that the habit of joining sign and thing signaled inappropriately, is amply illustrated. But the misperception occurs only in a particular context: prolonged, habitual fear.

We can put it in pictorial terms: in the foreground, dominant, is the veteran scrambling under the bed when the car backfires. A misreading of circumstances.

The source of this mis-reading is fear, found in the middle ground. We can imagine causes of the fear, even visualize the physiological changes the body undergoes in this state of terror.

The last field, the background, can be viewed as history, which informs middle and foreground.But history loosely-defined, for though the events did occur in time past these may not be remembered, may have undergone various transformations like exaggeration, switching of roles, or other alterations.

A reminder: habits are formed, become encapsulated by the murder of memory. Keeping this in mind, let's return to our painting.

Now the background must be vague, a melange of ill-defined incidents but with key events sharply rendered, (think Turner) yet unavailable because they're encapsulated within a membrane (think Bosch).

So: events triggered fear, an appropriate response; to

avoid the pain of that fear it was enveloped, leading to a free-floating anxiety no longer attached to the initiating cause, but with concommitant body symptoms lying in wait for an event to trigger their expression. In the foreground, this event occurs, and action results which is consistent with the bodily symptoms but not with the precipitating signal.

But wait, you say, doesn't James assert the proper order is: see bear—run—*then* feel afraid? Whereas your veteran is seeing bear, feeling fear, running. Is not your picture scrambled? Precisely. It's Post-traumatic-stress-*disorder,* not PTS *order.*

To further complicate things, psychologists have determined that there are two kinds of remembering: the purely cerebral, and a kind of re-living wherein both psychological and physiological components are fully expressed no matter how many times the memory recurs. We might call this habit-exclusive, since the experience is *not* deprived of memory, and each time the memory returns it is re-lived as though it were the first time. Zen mind, beginner's mind.

To return to our model: source-events to fear to enactment of fear. Now the complications: source-events, because of their indefinition and envelopment, are unavailable. Their effect, the fear, unattached from its origination, free-floats, the lack of reference rendering it as useless for sustaining equilibrium between the organism and its environment (remember Dewey?) as a fibrillating heart.

The organism remains in a state of panic, unassociated, unapproachable, unassailable.

•　•　•　•

I rarely see the homesteaders anymore. Their support, though often nebulous and always problematical because their solutions never swerved from the eye-for-eye, tooth-for-tooth type, still gave me the illusion of not being entirely alone. Now, on the rare occasions I do see them they no longer ask what's happening and if I volunteer information they change the subject. With Bettina, too, relations are prickly, not only because she also would like a final "shoot-out" but because I have given her advice about her son which angered her. Of course I know better than to advise, but in this case the stakes were so high (her son's health) that I felt I had no choice. Worse yet, she refuses to acknowledge her anger with me so it appears surreptitiously in actions.

As in the past when I have chosen to recognize that I am alone, that there is no source for help, I feel, unaccountably, greatly strengthened. I no longer dissipate energy by turning in the wind. I stand calm, and secure, in my aloneness.

Not regretting, but assessing, I think of responses I might have made which could have proved more effective. Some I actually considered doing, but when I would voice them to my "supporters" they were unacceptable because they were unorthodox, sometimes outrageous, and my supporters were wedded to the orthodox. The outrageous remark or action, was a valued part of my family armamentarium, particularly necessary for atheists in biblebelt country. As I mentioned, our unspoken rule was to be pleasantly accomodating up to the point, unmistakable, where push became shove. Then the outrageous word or action, never combative, was brought into play. And because it issued from energy created in the instant, guileless and unedited, its effect uncalculated, it resulted in not only clearing the air but astonishing opponents into receptivity, albeit momentarily and, not the least, restoring your own sense of self and the power that that engenders.

She remembers as a Fullbright Scholar in Germany her dismay when, expecting to find a "homeland". she had instead seemed to meet only hostility. And had finally deciphered this puzzle as being their resentment when they recognized—here it was again—that she was free and celebrating it. It could not be her clothes which, purposefully, echoed their own drab conventional wear; not her manner, generally modest and quiet. But her walk ah, that was a different matter entirely. For it was the walk of an animal who was in love with movement for its own sake, the walk of a creature who was immeasurably pleased with the world and her place in it. The walk of one who observed everything and took delight in the seeing; who, for sheer joy, sang or whistled as she moved.

And it was when she walked on the streets of Freiburg (ha!) that the people stopped and glared at her, the women gesturing, pointing at her while making comments to their companions, not even bothering to disguise their disapprobation. For there too, freedom was an important word and concept, but the practice of it verboten. When this disapproval begin to eat away at her, the "solution" came out of that family history of outrageous acts, not the specific choice of act but the device.

Thereafter, as she moved down the street, she would bark and growl at those who openly displayed hostility. Walking along, now whistling, now growling like a Doberman, then yipping like a Terrier, now singing Bach, never breaking stride, making each transition sound utterly natural and never, after the first experiment, glancing back to see the effect. For what she saw that once pleased her immensely; people, some alone, some in groups of two or three, frozen in consternation. Like statues they stood, incapable of sound or fury. This bestowed on her a wonderful sense of immunity and power.

Some of the acts she had contemplated: in peaked hat and straw wig, riding a broomstick down the main street in full daylight, looking neither to right or left; showing up at the Baptist Church one Sunday morning to sit smiling through the service then still wearing a beatific smile, leave; painting WITCH on a number of selected mailboxes or porch-posts one dark night, so that in this climate, where blame was assigned willy-nilly to whomever one despised most at the moment, a great busyness would descend, a kind of civil war and she would reap the benefit of their distraction.

But those moments of ripeness had passed. Such acts require a kind of energy no longer available to her. A necessary energy for what is being put on the line then, is not only your beliefs, your freedom, but your very life.

March 16, 1989
While I am gone today G. cuts down five large trees, arranging so they fall across my driveway. As I return, he is just putting his chain-saw into the bed of his truck which he has parked on my property. Make complaint to the new sheriff who at the suggestion of Kingroe, comes out and takes pictures.

March 18, 1989
See sheriff to express my fears about G. retaliating when he receives summons for my small-claims suit.
Sheriff D. says, "Look, you don't have to let him harm you but if you have to shoot him, act like you're scared."
I stare at him. *Act* like I'm scared. Tell him I've been scared every minute, every second, for three years.

March 20, 1989
Increasingly nervous about the delay in serving summons, I've contacted the court several times. They can't/won't explain the unusual delay but do tell me Judge M. will not sit the case—they won't say why—conflict of interest or what. This judge bears the same last name as the commissioner I've dealt with about the road. Most people here are related either by blood or marriage so it would seem certain those having the same name are related.

She lies awake, as usual. As is her habit now, she tries to think of practical tasks, chores associated with daily living which require nothing but the expenditure of physical energy. She has long given up the effort of trying to work intellectually or creatively.

Well, was there enough wood to last through the winter or should she order more? But wait, is this fall or spring? She closes her eyes and tries to remember being outside that day and what the weather had been like. Was she wearing a jacket? But she can't remember. Well then, go back to the beating. That was August, hot, start from there. Then the Lt. Governor, the mediation—that was December, then .... what? Oh, all the lawyers she'd seen. So this must

100

be spring. March. Or April.

❂   ❂

Crouching in the tall grass, frozen in mind and body, she is a quivering monument. No longer does she hop away when she sniffs out the cat waiting to pounce. Nor does she flee in front of the barking dogs. Nose and tail trembling, ears flickering to each sound, she keeps her eyes lowered for the deep humiliation of the beating, and its condoning, which has declared her despicable. Worthless. Dispensable.
She waits.

•   •   •   •

William James' father, Henry, was accidently burned during his childhood, requiring amputation of one leg above the knee. We may speculate that this had a profound effect and most likely factored in his decision to become a minister. However, after attending Princeton Theological Seminary he developed an antipathy to all eccliasticisms. When William was two, though, his father discovered Swedenborg, and this learned man of science gave him much solace, particularly in his doctrine that God is not a personality, but infinite Divine love and wisdom. From then forward Henry dropped every vestige of anthropomorphism in his religion and became completely spiritual. The vision he fashioned was a combination of the spiritual and the intellectual, which ambience he set forth abundantly at tea and dinner. Though father and son disagreed on many particulars, it seems evident in reading *Varieties Of Religious Experience,* published when William was sixty, that his conclusions regarding religion (i.e. assessing its effects, and its utilitarian aspect as the primary criteria) was but the flowering of those seeds ingested with the family tea and cakes.

•   •   •   •

101

Triangulation, a term used both in navigation and surveying, is a method of determining where you are on earth by the establishment of a fixed point in the sky. In essence, you cannot know where here is, you are, until you know where there is.

She stands alone in the field, then steps off, roughly, a distance of twenty feet from a fence-post, marks the spot with a stone, returns and nails the target to the fence-post.

I get the gun from the back of the closet. I have forgotten everything—how to load it, how to hold it, how to aim, how to fire. I ask my tenant, a Viet Nam veteran, how to do these things.

Then each day at one-o'clock, I put in ear-plugs, get the gun, walk to the rock, fire twenty shots at the target. My limbs move like a soldier or an automaton, my stomach remains clenched like a fist throughout the exercise.

After a week I am hitting the target on all shots and two of four are centered.

After two weeks, though I still move like a robot and my stomach remains in a spasm throughout, I no longer carry the gun at arm's length. I am still rigid with fear and revulsion but I am no longer afraid of the gun.

Habitually now, I hit the bulls-eye four out of five shots. I am ready. But ready for what, I do not know.

March 31, 1989

G. has trespassed almost every day this week, snipping limbs off trees, cutting small cedars, doing this for hours every day while I watch from the house. Mostly he is where I can see him, but then he will move to the back where there are no windows and I get very uneasy until he comes into sight again. He never appears to be looking at the house and I used to think he was unaware or uncaring, but I know now that it is cunning. His sight is better than mine and he carefully positions his body so that he can observe without appearing to do so. And every day he moves a little closer to the house.

Today he is back again cutting in my yard, using loppers. It is time.

I go out with the gun, shout his name. He looks up and sees me, then resumes cutting. I fire the gun into the air. Again he looks up, again resumes cutting. It is as though I don't exist. I am hesitant, realize I should have had a plan which would take into account this eventuality. I had been counting on the mere fact of my appearing with a gun being as earth-shattering an event for him as it is for me. Now he slowly begins walking towards me, loppers in hand. I back up, close to the porch steps then, while he is still some twenty feet away, I fire to the side of him, hitting a small branch. He stands there, apparently quite calm.

"Go ahead and shoot me," he says.

I can't understand why he doesn't seem the least afraid. Is something in my behaviour telling him he is safe? Why is he so sure when I myself am not? Is he basing it on past experience with me? But I've never had a gun in my hand before.

I look at him and know that I cannot shoot. He must recognize this.

I am suddenly so very tired. And, unaccountably, think of my mother.

Very calmly he says that now he will go get his gun and kill me. It is as though we are caught in an ancient drama, reenacting it in slow motion.

I am not sure who moves away first. But suddenly I feel a great urgency. Two monstrous facts loom: I cannot shoot him but he will shoot me. I run into the house, call the sheriff and say there's been a shooting. I make sure the cats are in the house and that all the windows closed and doors locked then realize I cannot stay here for I am too frightened.

I get into my car and drive to the sheriff's office. Before I get out of the car I see that I have put the gun on the seat beside me. I'm not sure what to do with it. Recall something about concealed weapons being illegal so I can't hide it under the seat or in the glove compartment, can I? But if I leave it on the seat it may go off by itself. If I unload it, then can I put it under the seat?

But now I realize that though I cannot use the gun, neither can I do without it. Yet I can't carry it into the sheriff's office. And now I find I can't even touch it, can't unload it. Something in my mind breaks loose, enormous waves engulf me. My brother, my father, I think of them. I think of other men in my life who, almost exclusively, have felt protective towards me and how I enjoyed *feeling* protected though I never wanted to be actually protected.

But there are no brothers, fathers, lovers or husbands here and when I reach the sheriff, having left the gun on the seat, my need is apparently so obvious that he, momentarily, does act protective. He tells me that a deputy is either on his way to my house or has arrived. He does not ask me what happened. Indeed, he shows me the pictures he took of the downed trees and asks me to indicate on the survey map where the trees were.

Finally I ask if he doesn't want to hear what happened. He shrugs his shoulders, it seems this is just another episode to him, no different than the cutting of the trees. I am not asked to write anything.

When we are finished, I realize I have no place to go. I cannot go home yet there is no other place. I ask if the deputy found G. near my place with a gun. Though he has reported in, it's not clear where he found G., though he has spoken with him. I ask, knowing it futile, if I can have protection. I ask if the deputy is still in the area of my house so that I can at least get into my house without being shot. There are no answers.

I drive around aimlessly for a time but realize my fear is growing rather than subsiding, so start home. When I reach my road, I see a sheriff's car turn into it ahead of me so I drive fast to get into my house while it is still nearby. I see it is the sheriff, parked on my road in front of my house. He and G. are on the road talking. They talk for a long time, then walk to where G. was cutting when I came out with the gun. They then walk back to the sheriff's car, he spreads a map on his hood and points out some things to G.

After a long period, G. gets in his truck and leaves, I go out to the sheriff who tells me that now he has shown G. on the map that he was indeed on my property, he believes G. understands and won't bother me again. I look into the sheriff's face and see he is, indeed, sincere. So it's stupidity. For which there's no remedy.

April 17, 1989

I learn today by calling the court that G. was served with summons two days ago and court date is set for June 16. This is *not* a litigious people. Court dates for small-claims are usually within 10 days of filing; mine has taken almost three months.

And the promised warning when G. was served? I have such a strong sense of sinister machinations fomenting behind the scenes and this, plus my concern that G. has a whole month yet to act out his anger impels me to go see Kingroe and make a final request for protection.

But he's not in his office. I leave the building and am getting into my car when the sheriff drives up. I wave at him but he motions me over to his car, tells me I am under arrest and I should get in my car and follow him to his office. I think this not a very funny joke, but do drive the couple of blocks behind him, and we go into his office where he hands me a copy of the Miranda Rights. I can't find my glasses so he reads them to me. I am told that bail has been set at $30,000, and that if I can get a bond I can leave and would then be arraigned the next day. If I do not get a bond, then I will be arraigned this afternoon—it is now about ten in the morning. I have only a very vague idea of the meaning of any of these terms: bond, bail, arraignment, but want the latter to happen as soon as possible to clear up this terrible mistake—so I say I'll wait. The sheriff seems embarrassed, not knowing what to do with me. He is also angry and apologizes for my "getting the shaft". I am put in a hallway, behind a locked door, at the foot of stairs which lead up to the jail proper. There is a pay phone here on the wall but no place to sit except the stairs. A strong smell of rancid grease pervades and I wonder what I, a vegetarian, will eat should I be put in jail.

I sit on the bottom step and try to think what to do, who I should call. Finally call Bettina because I can't think of anyone else. Don't ask her to do anything because I don't know anything that can be done. But I'm thinking that someone on the outside should know I'm in here—just in case. I realize that if they can arrest me, they can do anything to me. Bettina questions why I would be arrested at all and particulary so long—seventeen days—after the incident. If, indeed, that's why I've been arrested. And is it merely coincidence that it occurs at the time of G.'s summons? She promises to come and I sit back down on the step to wait.

The sheriff unlocks the door to go up the stairs. He is accompanied by the commissioner who threatened me about the road and who, I'm sure, is aware of everything that's happening. He's the one who shares the judges last name. The commissioner nods at me with a half-smile I can't interpret, but which is not triumphant. This upsets me even more. Two reasons why he's *not* feeling triumphant jump into my mind: their plan for me is going so smoothly that complacency is warranted, or *what* will happen to me now is worse than he bargained for.

Despite reminding myself that arrest procedures are designed to make one feel deeply humiliated, this is precisely what I feel. And many unanswerable questions assail me. Someone must have tipped off the sheriff that I was leaving the courthouse for him to be waiting. Kingroe? Is that why he "wasn't there"? His secretary? But someone had to order her to do so. How many people are in on this?

106

Because even if the sheriff is "on my side", he still will do anything the prosecutor tells him to—like arresting me. What exactly *can* they do? Has all this been carefully arranged, including the delay in setting the court date? Does this mean the court, itself, is in on it?

I know records can be destroyed, I recall now that I was never told why I was arrested, there's no record of that happening, don't they take the prisoner's fingerprints after they're arrested? But those, too, could be destroyed.

I'm coming up on something I'm not ready to face: I could "disappear". I could "commit suicide". Bettina is the only one who knows I'm here and they could tell her they released me, don't know where I went. I suddenly recall an incident which appeared in the local paper the year before; a local lawyer's body had been found in the alley behind his office. He had been shot twice. Results of the police investigation: suicide. When this was questioned, due to the fact that the gun was found several blocks away and the coroner had declared both shots fatal, the explanation was that members of the lawyer's family had come upon the body and to hide the "shame" of suicide had carried the gun away. So I know that even a wildly concocted story about my death will pass.

Well, should I call a lawyer? But who? A bad lawyer, or one related to those in the conspiracy would be worse than none. At this point the sheriff unlocks the door again to tell me that if I decide to call a bondsman, he can give me the name of one who will charge less than the going rate. In my naiveté, I think this very nice of him—and it answers another question. Apparently I'm not expected to give the whole $30,000. but only part of it. This still doesn't make it more possible.

The bailiff brings me a cup of coffee, makes a pleasant remark. Everyone seems uncomfortable with my being here. Somehow I don't fit. Yet here I am.

The bailiff comes back and says the sheriff wants to put me in one of the offices. This gives me easy access, via the corridor, to the main door out. It crosses my mind that should I start out that door they have a good excuse to shoot me. Indeed later, when Bettina comes, bringing a friend, we freely come and go out of the building without interference, Bettina remarking that for someone so dangerous as to require $30,000. bail they are curiously lax about my escaping.

Shortly before the arraignment is to begin, the sheriff asks if I want to see a lawyer for a few moments. I feel reprieved, then try to think of how I can present the past three years coherently in a "few" moments. I despair. Besides,does not everyone protest innocence, claim frame-up?

But when I see the lawyer, Public Defender it turns out, I feel hope for the first time. He is overweight though not grossly so,rumpled,disheveled—and quick-thinking,direct and solid. He obviously knows what he's doing and, small miracle, can take charge.

"I just glanced through your file quickly," he says "and really, all this is very fishy. The charge oughta be dropped but probably all I can do for you now is get your bail reduced. $30,000.! ridiculous — and for someone who's never been charged before, well, I'll try to get it down to ten..."

He leaves then and much time passes before I am led into the courtroom by the bailiff. The Public Defender motions me to sit next to him at a table in front of the judge, then leans towards me and speaks very softly.

And a moment occurs, a moment of intimacy which I realize I have longed for so intensely for so long that tears come to my eyes, my breath catches. For isn't this what intimacy is—this leaning in towards someone, this purposeful physical closeness, this lowered voice saying: this is meant only for you, you, because at this moment I am thinking only of you and this means you are intrinsically valuable to me now, you, specifically in this moment are worthy of my full attention and my efforts now, in this moment. And for this brief time, a kind of love suffuses me, blushes and dampens my skin. I lean towards him, my body irresistibly moving, my posture duplicating his.

"This is even fishier than I thought," he whispers. "The judge and the prosecutor are adamant about not reducing bail." He moves even closer, I close my eyes.

"The judge said 'these two have been feuding a long time so we gotta do something before someone gets hurt'."
Now I hear only "...prejudicial remarks, disqualify himself, should but..." Then he approaches Kingroe, who has been studiously avoiding my eyes.
The judge calls my name. I stand before him and Kingroe reads the charge, which I am hearing for the first time. "...Class felony assault in the first degree that on or about March 31, she did attempt to kill or cause serious injury to J.G. by..."
"But that's not true!" I blurt out.
The judge gives a tenuous smile, murmurs something, then says, "Bail is set at $10,000."
The Public Defender pulls me to the side and says that while he would like to defend me this would require a hearing wherein I'd have to request a court appointed lawyer, time-consuming, but he can give me the name of a lawyer who is experienced and can easily handle this. I take the name. Back in the sheriff's office I ask which bondsman I should call.
"Oh," he splutters, looking at the deputies standing around, "you can call any of them—there's a list by the pay phone there."
I'm confused but go to the phone where he follows and points out a name. Then I understand.
The bondsman comes, looking and sounding just as they're portrayed in the movies, I give him a check for $300. and I am free to go.

April 17, 1989
I see the lawyer, Novak, recommended by the Public Defender, and despite many misgivings, retain him. The misgivings are: with his radio loudly playing a baseball game he asks me to tell him, in as few words as possible, about the case. One ear cocked towards the radio, he impatiently drums his fingers on his desk. He says he will not in any way implicate the prosecutor since he tries many cases in that county. When I point out that it is the sheriff's and prosecutor's failure to act on my behalf that compelled me

to protect my own property, he will not commit himself. He says he will try to get a dismissal of charges and when I tell him of my plans to leave the state he says, good, the court might be more inclined to dismiss if they know that. I tell him Kingroe *is* aware of my intentions, and that I absolutely would not accept my leaving as a condition for dismissal. He says his fee for dismissal will be $2000., if it goes to trial it will be $3000 or perhaps more. I write a check for $2000.

May 19-22, 1989
Novak calls to say preliminary hearing has been advanced to June 7 rather than June 21. He says this is highly unusual (I learn later that he *requested* the change in order for it not to interfere with his vacation) and I wonder aloud if the fact that this places it before, rather than after, the small-claims date is pertinent. He also tells me he called Kingroe and told him I was willing to leave the state if charges are dropped. So he was listening to the ballgame after all. I tell him this places the court in conspiracy with G. to "run me out" and that since he proposed it, against my expressed wishes, it places him, too, in conspiracy. He yawns and says, well, they haven't accepted it yet.
A couple of days later, after some consideration, I call Novak and fire him.
I see another lawyer but she says she will never again have anything to do with this court and particularly Judge M. who will be sitting for the preliminary. She's had innummerable run-ins with him and says this would compromise my case. Refers me to Alden, whom I see and retain.

⚙   ⚙

The county seat, where the court sits, is a town of 10,000 with, as might be expected in this part of the country, innumerable churches, mostly of the fundamentalist persuasion. A town of little or no grace, replete with Walmarts, K-Marts and an array of fast food emporiums.

Residences are tucked into whatever space is left over, giving the odd impression that Burger King, Kentucky Fried Chicken, Gospel of True Believers, came first, followed by the people.

Since the advent of the mall at the edge of town, the main street struggles, with empty stores and ones plastered with Going out of Business signs. A number of burned-out shells, the preferred solution to business woes, are seen regularly. Driving or walking through the town one gets an overwhelming impression of the driving force here: greed.

As might be expected, public service jobs are undertaken with this same theme in mind. The main selling points in campaigns and routinely mentioned, is the candidates religious affiliation, the fact that he/she is a native of the town and references to family, with the hopeful photographed formally, en famille. Being a native is meant to be interpreted, in case one should be ignorant of the fact, that the candidate has plenty of relatives serving in various capacities.

These public offices, mayor, sheriff, clerk, commissioners, prosecutor, are for the more ambitious citizen, and graft is an expected component of the office. But we speak here of graft in lowercase letters for it is limited by the amount available in a small town and by the imagination of the office holder. It is possible though, if a man has a long enough reign, say twelve years as a county sheriff, to build a substantial empire, derived from such things as recovery, and subsequent sale of stolen goods (auto and farm implements being prized) and various other extortion schemes.

❁   ❁

May 31, 1989
Alden is a lawyer entering private practice after a stint of being Assistant Prosecutor in a county south of here. A tall, loosely-jointed man, his humor, which appears rarely and suddenly, a surprise and delight. He is not sure of me, responding to my humor a beat or two late. Nor is he quite

convinced of my veracity, though there is a willingness to believe, and I accept this. We quickly establish a sense of trust and liking for each other. Reciting yet again the grueling account of the past years (this time with no competition from a ballgame), when I speak of the treachery of the other lawyer, Alden responds gently by saying that, considering the circumstances, and that court, this might be the best we can hope for.

I look out the window. It is impossible. For I know I cannot, it's not a case of *will* not, agree to bargain with a corrupt court even if it means I go to jail for 15 years. My respect and trust grows when Alden, without my saying anything —apparently my silence and tears have told him— indicates we'll try for unconditional dismissal. This will become our mode of operation with each other: he will present the obvious, easy route, but if I disagree, he will push harder, make more effort to gain a more satisfactory result for both of us. It's a good arrangement for it means I serve as monitor, necessarily having a voice and sharing responsibility for the outcome.

In the beginning of her trials the director jealously guarded her privacy, revealing circumstances only to those from whom she sought help. But with better perspective she realizes that what is happening to her must also be happening to others in similiar settings. Should she, for whatever reason, become unavailable to the locals, they would simply choose a replacement. For people like these need a scapegoat. Indeed, she has heard stories which suggest she is not the first "victim" here. She recognizes she must broadcast her own story—lest secrecy provide the environment for such incidents to flourish.

There was a great variety of responses to her story. As mentioned, there were the tsk-tskers, who either from a lack of imagination or to excuse themselves from involvement, could not react with emotional resonance. For others, the story triggered a memory in their own life, some injustice which still smoldered and would burst into flame, the conflagration relating to their own history, not hers.

There were those who saw her prolonged terrorisation as little more than an annoyance, a pimple unworthy of serious consideration. This made her doubt herself. Was she over-reacting? In the general scheme of things, the world filled with atrocities, should she not just take this in stride without complaint?

And then there were the ones upon whose faces registered, as she proceeded with her story, increasing disbelief. And she understood. For were she presented with such a story, she would find it difficult if not impossible to believe, or would assume there had been provocation. Would question why any law official, no matter how corrupt, in the face of such trangressions would persist in inactivity. What was there for them to gain? And so, identifying with her audience, she would falter, over-explain, for all the world look like the liar they took her to be, and leave the encounter feeling even more helpless, frustrated and humiliated.

There were some who reacted with strong indignation but their solutions were ones she could not accept.

But then her luck changed. She started attending a small Unitarian-Universalist Fellowship in a town fifty miles away, and after only a couple of months, trusted these dozen people enough to apprise them of what was happening.

From that time forward the kind of support which anticipated my wants and needs, where there was no separation between giver and receiver hence no feeling of obligation, this was mine. Though I sometimes feared that, like past support, this might prove ephemeral, that I would be left dangling and bruised, this never happened. They never presented me with " solutions" I found unconscionable for we were likeminded in our philosophy; they were, simply, *there.*

And they were there for me too when I went to court. Available when I called and if I did not call, they called me. My indignation and sense of injustice, theirs, my fears, theirs. And this made all the difference. They allowed me my independence, from which I derived my strength; I was supported, from which I also derived strength.

June 5, 1989
Though Novak had said the preliminary hearing had been advanced to June 7, Alden is told by the court it is still scheduled for the 21st. He calls Novak who insists he was notified of this change, so Alden thinks we had better be prepared and appear on the 7th in case the court is pulling some trick. So we meet today for several hours.

It proves to be a very difficult time, recounting details of all the incidents, pages and pages of them. I have repeated them so many times I feel they're engraved on my brain, and I alternate between extreme boredom and harrowing moments of re-living. Alden mentions Kafka and several times bursts out with, "Jesus, he oughta be sued," referring to G. My anger on the other hand has, I realize, been predominantly with the officials. When we get to the beating I start to hyperventilate so we take a break. We come back and I make it through this time without breaking down.

Twice we go over the shooting. Where was I when I fired the first shot in the air? Where were we in relation to each other when I fired the shot to the side of him? He tells me to take some pictures and bring them to court tomorrow, using a stand-in for G. to show where he was in relation to me, and then where I was in relation to him when I fired the shot. He tries to lead me with his questions.

"When he walked towards you with the loppers was he holding them up like a weapon? Are you sure the shot you fired hit a twig *only* 8-9 feet away from him—that's kind of close?"

I recognize what he is doing and I consider lying—after all, what difference does it make, we know where the guilt lies in all this — but, despite the pleading in his eyes, I do not. Mostly, I think, because I feel it unnecessary. I know what my intent was though Alden, obviously, isn't sure. I would like to help him with this but don't know how. Because of our misgivings about the hearing and subsequent trial if charges aren't dismissed, the U.U. people and I contact various agencies. Again I appeal to the ACLU, this time the St. Louis Chapter. They merely refer me back to the KC Chapter, who doesn't return my calls. To the local chief of the FBI, I explain we feel there's been a denial of due process, collusion on the part of law officials, false arrest. But the Chief claims that none of these would fall under the jurisdiction of the FBI. Asked if they can monitor or just be a presence at a courtroom hearing when there are indications of mishandling, he says this is outside their interest. When asked under what circumstance, precisely, they would become involved, he replys in a bored voice that if there had been police brutality and I had proof of this. We also appeal to the Freedom from Religion Foundation and it seems for a time they will become active on my behalf, but the final determination is that this doesn't fall under their purview of church-state separation.

Other appeals are made: to the director of an artists colony, a woman I haven't met but whom I know to be responsive, in an immediate and intelligent way, to injustice; a friend in New York with a friend who has a friend in the Justice Department, a friend in Vermont who knows someone in her local chapter of the ACLU, another friend in California with a history, hence possible contacts in, political activism. All respond warmly but can offer no practical help.

So on June 7 there are no White Horses galloping into the courtroom, their Noble Riders avenging the wrongs, then lifting me aloft and carrying me off to a finer, gentler world. There is only Alden, loaded with tape-recorder and notes, prepared as he said, to cross-examine G. an hour, two, as long as the court allows, in a way that he will never forget. And my U.U. friends, who had to get up very early to drive the 60 miles here by 8 AM; my two witnesses, one of whom has perhaps jeopardized his job by taking this day off; and Bettina, with whom I'd spent the previous afternoon. She has been very nervous about the courtroom proceedings, almost as though she herself is on trial, so we went over the written testimony I had collected from her at various times during the past three years. Then I had played inquisitor. But Bettina claimed she couldn't remember much of what she had witnessed, her written testimony didn't seem to jog her memory and, what was even worse, she kept making up things, blurting them out, each statement seeming designed to give lie to my testimony or even incriminate me. I point this out and she says she's so flustered she no longer knows what she's saying. I get increasingly anxious and angry, she gets increasingly adamant. It is too much for me and I am very unkind, screaming at her that she's either dumb or playing dumb— does she want me to go to jail? She's my prime witness after all, having been present for many incidents whereas my other witness has been present for only a few. We go then to take the pictures Alden requested, both still very angry. First Bettina, then I, serve as a stand-in for G. It feels eerie. I measure with a tape-measure and discover the shot I fired to the side of G. was, in fact, the 11-12 feet Alden suggested. And the distance between us at this point less than I thought. In this re-enactment, I've discovered that which will relieve Alden of his doubts.

In the courtroom, I introduce Alden to the witnesses. Bettina's behaviour as we drove in together has only increased my anxiety about her witnessing so I've decided to apprise Alden of the situation and let him decide whether to use her. I hand the snapshots to him and make some quip about them. Already at some distance from this drama unfolding around me, my self-of-substance slowly ascends to safety near the vaulted ceiling while my surrogate self, instincts intact, remains below. The two will not again merge until this is over.

· · · ·

In the spring of 1907, William James repeated lectures given before at Harvard and Columbia. His subject, pragmatism, was much misunderstood by the general public. Wherever he lectured though, evidence of his popularity was the size of his audiences, numbering in the hundreds, then thousands, people turned away at the door. For James was an unusual, charismatic personage. Beloved by his students, respected and admired by colleagues, friends all over the world in all different languages, treasured by his family, he rode this vessel of affection with confidence and a strong sense of responsibility. Note too, that such interest was the mark of another era. Would thousands attend any talk today dealing with the nature of truth?

James had, for some years, been troubled with angina, exacerbated his doctors thought, by his insistence on hiking in the mountains, occasionally getting lost and spending the night. Ever the peripatetic, his last long journey into death was a tortuous one. Now suffering with violent heart pain from the slightest exertion or upset, he nevertheless makes the voyage to Henry in England. For Henry, experiencing a nervous breakdown, has summoned him, and William, ever the big brother, follows his inclination, arriving at Rye in March, 1910. The various treatments he undergoes that summer for his heart condition all prove ineffective so he, Alice and Henry embark for home.

Leaving Rye at noon on August 11, they reach a rainy London at four, stay in a hotel that night, leave for Euston Station the next morning and at 4 PM William is carried on board a ship where, for the next five days, he is too tired to rise from his berth. Arriving at Quebec on the 6th day, Alice's terse journal indicates he is "very suffering" and that "everything begins to go wrong."

"Arrive at 4" the journal continues, "Harry, (their son who is to escort them on the next leg of their journey) furious rain, horrid hotel. Wm. walking too much, very bad night, awake and dressing at 4 AM, customs, Wm. sick there, long and terrible day traveling. Reach Intervale at 6 PM, Billy (another son who will drive them the last

117

lap), motor, home.

By the time they reach Chocorua, William's beloved country home, his feet are badly swollen, indicating his condition so worsened that fluids are collecting in his body.

But he has reached home.

Family and relatives fill the house shortly, but Alice allows no one else but herself to attend to William for the next six days. Days of great pain, doctors visits, failed remedies.

At the last, knowing he is dying, William makes a solemn request that Alice also attend Henry "when his time comes." That same night Alice records: "Wm. dies just before 2:30 in my arms. I was just coming into the room with his milk and saw the change. No pain at the end and no consciousness. He had had morphine continously since Wednesday."

She lifted his head from the pillow and was holding it when the end came. "Wonderful beauty of dear face," she recorded two days later.

. . . .

We learn that I am not on the docket for today, the hearing still scheduled for June 21. But Alden says the time won't be wasted, he'll talk to Kingroe about dismissal. The prosecutor himself is nowhere to be seen. Alden beckons me into the hall and under the stairs, the only place with relative privacy. I tell him I appreciate that intent (to kill) is the trickiest part of the charge. He moves closer. I tell him of my practice with the target and the degree of proficiency I'd reached.

"Do you mean..."

"When I took the pictures I measured the distance. It was only fourteen feet. I could easily have hit him."

He nods. But something still bothers him. I think I know what it is.

"He didn't act threatening with the loppers because, see, the most remarkable thing was that he *never* seemed the least bit afraid throughout ... As though he *knew* I wouldn't shoot him, something told him..."

118

"It *is* odd," he says, "people don't generally walk towards you after you've fired a warning shot—and when you're still holding the gun."

We look at each other, he nods. It is the first time he really believes, rather than *wanting* to believe, that I had no intent. We go back into the courtroom.

Now I am three people: the one needing protection still out of harm's way near the ceiling, the surrogate, actually in charge, and the observer of the surrogate. This observer notes that the surrogate appears quite calm and confident. Everything has assumed a surrealistic, uncanny quality, reflecting the three simultaneous perspectives and lending each event greater intensity, depth and size. And it seems these events unfold very slowly.

In this highly-charged atmosphere, much akin to acute sexual tension, every glance, gesture, movement, sound, nuance of conversation, takes on a deeply-engraved significance. There is the abiding love issuing from my friends, now seated in a corner of the small courtroom, to whom I return each time I've talked to Alden, to report what is going on. Like a child in the midst of strangers, venturing out from its parents, returning, venturing out. And I do feel childlike, taking my first steps, surrounded by an audience beaming at me which I keenly sense in my pre-verbal state. I am contained, floating in this sanctuary of pure energy. Remarkably, this same love-as-energy flows from Alden and in this oversensitized state we revert mostly to non-verbal communication, with consummate comprehension.

I don't see him talking with Kingroe, but "know" he is, and turn at the exact moment he finishes and signals me to follow him into the hall again. Of course we do not embrace nor even touch but there is a sense of coming together into intimacy. Anguish sits on his face and I shake my head no. They want you to leave, he confirms, they're afraid something will happen. I don't state the obvious. Incredibly, it seems their choice of who to prosecute has nothing to do with guilt, but who has resided here the longest, and our relative ages. Because I'm younger than G.,

I lose. Also he's a Baptist—and I am not. And they present this as though it's a cogent, defensible argument.

I have no choice, there is no painful decision to make, I whisper that I cannot put myself in conspiracy with my own victimization. He nods, says he'll talk to them again.

We go back into the courtroom where other business continues to be carried on in the front near the judge, while our drama unfolds in the back and in the hall. I squat before my friends and convey the news. And again know, rather than see, when Alden finishes his talk with Kingroe and beckons me into the hall, where he indicates we move even further under the stairs.

We stare at each other. He asks if I would accept a reduction of the charge to misdemeanor, disturbance of peace. I consider. More accurate, I think, for I *did* disturb the peace by firing the gun and am willing to accept that responsibility. But he reads my thinking and before I can acquiese, holds up his hand and says, let me talk to him some more.

Back in the courtroom. Another short consultation with Kingroe, again Alden meets my eyes, again I follow him into the hall. They'll give dismissal if you'll agree to pay court costs, he says, that would be $30-40.

No conditions?

No conditions, he replies.

I say yes.

When we return to the courtroom the judge calls me to the bench, asks if I'm willing to pay court costs, I say yes and consider tacking on "your honor" but cannot. "Case dismissed," he says.

Alden says, thank you, your honor, then immediately beckons me out into the hall again.

Had there been onlookers, deprived of the priviledge of sound, they could only have interpreted this exchange under the stairs as that of the desperate avowal of lovers. And in its most basic sense, that's what it is. I recognize it as a love born of necessity, unlimited in depth and real as stone, but finite in time, lasting only while need persists. And because I do recognize this, I can yield autonomy, allow myself the luxury of being swayed, buoyed up by this gift from the gods, this state of grace.

As we talk, the urgency of our conversation is matched by the urgency of feelings and our bodies move closer to each other, then away, to the side, following or resisting in an exquisite and tantalizing dance. I feel very alive. He says the court demands there be no more exchanges between G. and me.

I say, But I can't guarantee what G. will do—he'll be back, he will, *he will!*

Stay in the house, he says.

But then I'll be a prisoner.

If he comes, stay in the house, don't confront him. DON'T GO OUT!

What if he is destroying everything?

Then call the sheriff.

But when I simply gaze at him he realizes, leans very close says desperately and emphatically, then CALL ME!, We stare at each other, leaning in even closer, careful not to touch.

Stay in the house, he whispers.

I nod. Some vital piece of information, some admission from him has been granted me and I relax.

What about the civil suit? I ask.

No. no, he says, wait a while.

But I'll be going away.

Yes, he says, leave, then just come back for the court date. I need to know because of the small-claims suit. I can't do both.

I don't want to advise you, he says, but I'd drop it.

OK. But shouldn't we start on the civil suit?

He shakes his head. I won't start while you're still in the house and I don't want you here until you come back for the actual court date.

We look at each other, not quite ready yet.

Do you want me to write a letter to G., he asks.

Oh yes. Yes.

Can you stay with someone or have someone stay with you until you leave?

It's very awkward. But I will stay in the house.

He nods.

We are ready now. I offer my hand, we are very business-like. I thank him and go back into the courtroom where my friends are waiting. I am embracing and being embraced as Alden, unobserved by me, gathers his stuff and leaves.

O ne morning in June I drive away. I know I'll be returning on short, purposeful trips from time to time but this is essentially my farewell. For I will be returning as a visitor, a stranger even, my bond to these forests and gentle hills ripped asunder. At the top of one hill I pull the car over to do a kind of summing up of losses. The Colony, which I will not again establish, either here or elsewhere for I no longer have that kind of energy. My house, for whose design and construction I gave four years of my life and the same kind of devotion as would a symphony I wrote. This house, full of light and grace, will always be uninhabitable by me and by anyone else capable of enjoying its special beauty.

But both of these losses were at one time fully realized experiences, hence capable of being relinquished. I can let them go.

Far more troubling are the psychological losses. I believe these to be not merely wounds, capable of healing, but amputations. Gone is my profound, instinctive trust of others. Now, even with those I've known and loved before, there is an unsettling feeling that what I perceive might not be there, that what is there I may not be perceiving. This distrust of my own perceptions makes all relations so painful that I no longer know how to be with others. Like a barbed wire in the throat is this doubt. Far less painful is to believe, on first sight, that this person greeting me so warmly can, will, deceive me. In as instant.

Pavlov's dog. Habit is exactly conditioning, conditioning exactly habit.

Not recognized yet is the habitual state of fear my body

retains, encapsulated and inaccessible. Fear which is activitated by many visual and olfactory cues, sounds, such as a truck or tractor starting up or passing, or any unknown, unidentifiable sound in the night. And I continually lie in wait for these sights, smells and sounds to occur for the wisdom contained in that inaccessible capsule is that my very life depends on vigilance. Hence, bifurcated by past and present, much of myself consumed by a terror justified only by the past, my present and presence is become attenuated, diminished.

I start the car and drive slowly along a road as familiar to me as my hand. Early morning mist still clings to the lowlands. I see this through the mist of my tears. For I have loved and do love this land fiercely. And know it intimately. That path there leads over a rise to a small grove of trees where cows gather on windy winter days, and seek relief from the burning sun on long August afternoons. That stream, whose source I discovered one blustery March day, a spring slowly bubbling like a heart-beat, meanders through the field for several miles, runs over flat basalt, then drops in a perfect, miniature, waterfall. Enter those woods at the point where the dead hickory looms starkly, walk three quarters of a mile and you will find a mysterious clearing whose center contains a monumental white oak. Listen at night from your sleepless bed, to the whippoorwill's cry reverberating through the forest.

These, and many other secrets of this place are the things I know. And by the knowing, they are mine forever.

EPILOGUE

When I drove away that fine June morning I had planned to toss the gun into the Mississippi as I crossed it. A symbolic gesture. Ironies continued though. Driving placed me on the wrong side to throw anything over the rail, and because of traffic I could not stop and finally, there was no place on the bridge for pedestrians.

For a while I tried to settle in a medium-sized town in Northern Pennsylvania. But I had arrived too late. Beauty was still evident, in the gracious old Victorian homes, in the sparkling river dissecting the town, and in the surround of mountains, but destruction and decay were ever-gaining enemies. Families still frolicked in the Susquehanna but now had to lock their bicycles and watch their clothes.

And everywhere there was noise. During my ten years in the country where, before G.'s truck-starting became my wake-up call, dawn's greeting had been a rooster's crow from across the valley. Whereas city life, during my absence, had succumbed to a degree of habituation to noise undreamt of by me. Incessant traffic, violent rhythm pounding rap and rock, it filled the air, my lungs and ears, my head. There when I went to bed, and there when, for escape, I moved from bedroom to kitchen, to the bathroom and, finally, to a closet where it still pulsated, still threatened, but no longer smothered me.

And it was there, in the closet, where I felt safely enough removed from G., to begin my nightmares. They seemed a toxin my body needed to throw off in order to heal. So this poison, like the firecrackers on that July evening which now seemed so long ago, exploded nightly into visions.

Nor could my cats adjust. No longer did they move freely and arrogantly but cowered in cupboards, their eyes and coats dull. And though I pointed to those cats happily dozing on porches or lolling unconcerned under bushes

124

within feet of the traffic, they remained unconvinced. I conceded that cats, and perhaps people as well, must be to the melee born ...

I thought longingly of the Zen monastery. At some distance from the main building there were wood-stove heated cabins, used in part for an artist-in-retreat program. An ideal place, I thought, to work, participate in Zen training, have my cats, and heal myself. But the same monk to whom I had appealed before was as unresponsive this time. Yes, she said, if I could meet a couple of conditions both of which she was well aware I could not meet. First, my cats would not be allowed even though she, herself, kept a dog in the monastery and there were cats there as well. Secondly, she mentioned a monthly fee she knew I couldn't afford. It would seem the cloistered life fosters a degree of insensitivity.

So I moved myself to a small university town in Western New York where there was available. on the property of a friend, a summer youth camp now vacated. For it was October, winter approaching. Yet another irony, perhaps fitting, for this was a Baptist camp. Here I chilled myself thoroughly until rescued from the cold by Alden's message that, the summons having been served with no resulting fireworks, he deemed it safe for me to return, particularly since a friend who had been using my house would stay on for the first few critical weeks.

Hence in November I left the snow in New York and found Indian Summer in Missouri. Strangely enough, it was my friend who now had the nightmares which I, for the most part had left behind, awakening me at night with her strangled cries for help.

The nightmares were about G., she said. I didn't ask for details.

D r. C. enters the examining room and greets me. He doesn't have me quite in focus and I think he may be tired or that something in his day has gone awry—perhaps me. I worry because, only a few years in practice, he still becomes very involved with his patients and this, in certain eventualities, requires him to impose an emotional distance. My concern is that, to protect himself he will achieve a distance merely a step away at first, then the habit, like a cancer, will develop and grow until he sees his patients as though through the wrong end of a telescope. This will be intolerable—for him as well as his patients.

I try to measure his emotional distance. Once, I had joked with him that I knew before he spoke whether his news was good or bad. Surprised, he asked me how I knew. Simple, I said, when it's bad you walk in backwards. Today the distance is not as great as the time before last, but he is somewhat detached.

So I know he has bad news for me.

But we both want to stretch out this interim before the news is placed there, inescapable, irredeemable, between us.

As is his habit, there is physical contact, his body leaning against my shoulder, his hand on my knee. His is a touch which fills the gaping voids left by the inadequacy of words. Or by words better left unspoken. It is this gift of touch which has carried me across the crevasses, which I have sought often in these past months and which has always been, without need for request, lovingly extended.

"What's been happening with you? Is there anything you want to tell me about?"

I hesitate. The words we put into this interval aren't important, merely something to stretch out the time. I mumble about general condition, he mumbles replies. His touch is working its magic: I am warmed, consoled, made ready. I ask if I'm crazy to be concerned about a particular symptom, if there is reason to think it more sinister than is apparent. He explains that if there is a lot of pain, it seems located in the bone and persists over a long period then yes, concern.

He turns his back slightly, picks up my chart, fumbles with but doesn't open it and I prepare myself.

"Your CEA is up," he says, not looking at me.

126

For the final irony, it seems, the ultimate treachery, taking place within this time, was the formation of a new habit, gone wild and wreaking destruction in a secret compartment of my body. Perhaps a desperate effort to provide me, in a no-way-out situation, an exit visa.

Never mind that twenty-two years of vegetarianism, an absence of family proclivity and a personal history absolutely devoid of precipitating factors, the organism followed that inexorable path, or habit, of moving from prolonged stress to compromised immune system to proliferation of aberrant cells to colon cancer.

At home again, my new home, I lie supine, again will my rational mind into oblivion, again demand of my right brain that it take the reins, enlisting my immune system to restore those functions I hope will become a firm habit.